£9

Branch Lines of
Devon

Exeter and South, Central and East Devon

Branch Lines of Devon

Devon

Exeter and South, Central and East Devon

COLIN G. MAGGS

Budding
BOOKS

A Budding Book

First published in 1995 by Alan Sutton Publishing Limited, an imprint of
Sutton Publishing Limited · Phoenix Mill · Thrupp · Stroud · Gloucestershire

This edition published in 1998 by Budding Books,
an imprint of Sutton Publishing Limited

A catalogue record for this book is available from the British Library

ISBN 1 84015 022 X

Typeset in 9/10pt Palatino.
Typesetting and origination by
Sutton Publishing Limited.
Printed in Great Britain by
WBC Limited, Bridgend, Mid-Glamorgan.

Contents

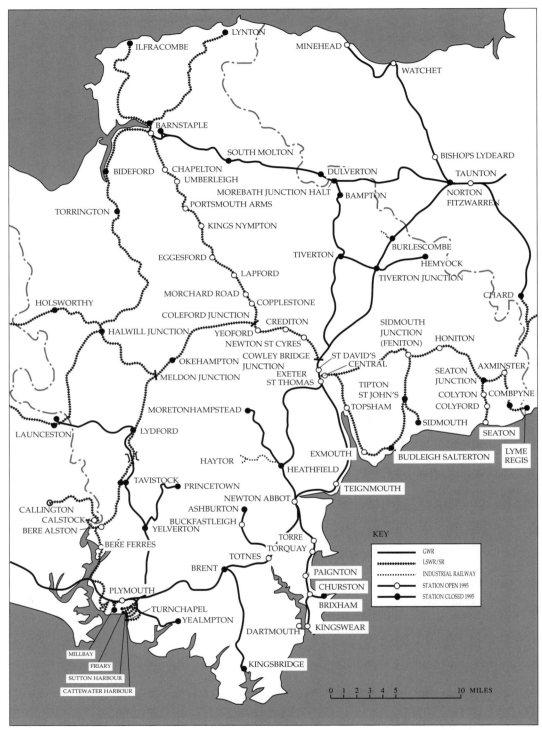

BRANCH LINES OF DEVON

Introduction

The railway map of Devon has a simple basic pattern. In the 1840s the allies of the broad gauge Great Western Railway, the Bristol & Exeter Railway and the South Devon Railway, thrust the main line forward to Plymouth. A number of places were off the route and in due course branch lines were built to serve them.

The broad gauge faction did not hold its monopoly for long. In 1860 the London & South Western Railway opened from Salisbury to Exeter to gain a share of the West Country traffic, offering a shorter, though more steeply graded route to London. Between Exeter and Axminster the LSWR thrust branches to the south coast, while the GWR covered the area north of the LSWR. From Exeter to Lydford matters were reversed, the LSWR serving the north and the GWR the south. Both companies had branches in the Plymouth area.

Some branches in Devon were considered main lines – the Norton Fitzwarren to Barnstaple branch being so marked by the GWR on its maps. The Newton Abbot to Kingswear branch for most of its life was a main line, but today can be considered a branch. The former LSWR between Exeter and Barnstaple used to be a main line, but is now relegated to branch status.

The GWR found that one advantage of keeping the broad gauge was that it deterred the LSWR from seeking running powers. Eventually, however, the cost and inconvenience of transhipment at the break of gauge caused the broad gauge line to be converted, the last of this work being carried out in May 1892. After the narrowing of the gauge there were at least two main routes between London, Exeter and Plymouth – a useful arrangement as when one was blocked through accident, landslip, storm or flood, trains could use the alternative.

As well as the main lines of the respective companies being used as alternatives, the GWR was able to utilize some of its branch lines to bypass a problem. If the coast line through Dawlish was blocked, the branch line from Newton Abbot through Heathfield to Exeter could be used, while an alternative route between Stoke Canon and Tiverton Junction was via Tiverton. Another way of reaching Norton Fitzwarren from Stoke Canon was through Dulverton. These branch line alternatives were not ideal as they had single track, weight restrictions which barred certain classes of locomotives, and sometimes a junction layout requiring a reversal.

The Bristol & Exeter Railway, which reached the county town in 1844, was not Devon's first permanent line. This honour was held by the Haytor Tramway. Opened in 1820, it carried granite to the Stover Canal where the stone was transhipped and taken to Teignmouth for transport by sea. In 1858 the tramway fell out of use, but part of its formation was used by the Moretonhampstead branch.

Although Devon lost many branches in the closures of the 1950s and 1960s, several

LSWR advert for Devon & Cornwall 1913.

remain open – those to Exmouth, Barnstaple, Paignton and Gunnislake – while preserved lines run to Buckfastleigh, Kingswear and Seaton.

Devon had so many branch lines that in order to deal with them adequately, two volumes are required. This, the first, deals with the LSWR branches in East Devon together with those of the GWR in the Exeter and Torbay areas. A second volume will cover the west of the county from the Plymouth district to the Barnstaple area.

In this volume ex-LSWR branches are described first and then those of the GWR. In both cases the sequence follows from east to west.

Grateful thanks are due to E.J.M. Hayward for checking and improving the text and captions.

Key to all maps:

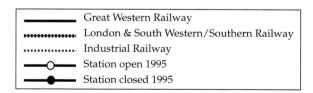

——————	Great Western Railway
++++++++++++	London & South Western/Southern Railway
··················	Industrial Railway
——○——	Station open 1995
——●——	Station closed 1995

Axminster to Lyme Regis

In the early 1760s a Lyme Regis innkeeper purchased a bathing-machine, the assembly rooms were opened and the town started its change from port to resort. Although three railway schemes were drawn up in 1845, nothing came of them; in fact nothing was done even after the Lyme Regis Railway cut its first sod so splendidly in 1874. Most of the trouble was caused by the people of Chard and Axminster, who argued over which town would make the best starting point, everyone patriotically wanting their own to be chosen.

In 1896 the government passed the Light Railways Act and this allowed some branches, subject to certain restrictions, to be built and worked more cheaply: level-crossing gates were not insisted upon and signalling could be simpler.

The Axminster & Lyme Regis Light Railway was promoted, the estimated cost of the 6¾ mile line being £49,938. An inquiry was held at Axminster on 1 February 1899 and a Light Railway Order granted on 15 June the same year. Arthur C. Pain was appointed engineer.

Baldry & Yerburgh's tender of £36,452 for building the line was accepted on 10 April 1900. The future looked rosy as £50,360 had been subscribed, including £25,000 from the LSWR, all shares being taken up by 5 July. The contractors started work on 21 June 1900 and the first seaborne cargo of materials for constructing the line was discharged in early August from the ketch *Ida* at the Cobb, Lyme Regis.

The work carried out by Baldry & Yerburgh did not go entirely without complication. One problem occurred as their railway engine was being hauled through a narrow lane at Trill, near Axminster, en route to the site. The engine became jammed between banks and these had to be cut away to release it.

The principal engineering work was the ten-arch Cannington Viaduct. This was one of the first viaducts to be constructed in concrete and when built by 'Concrete Bob' McAlpine was the second highest of its kind in England. It has a maximum height of 93 ft and a total length of 182 yd. Crushed flints from an adjacent cutting offered a suitable material for making concrete without sand, and the cement was brought by sea to the Cobb. To save costs, a cableway was used instead of scaffolding. Unfortunately one of the arches started slipping a fortnight before the line was due to be opened. This delayed the inauguration and caused additional expense. It also spoilt the symmetry of the viaduct as a jack arch had to be inserted to support the weakened structure. For the first three years after opening a watchman was posted to keep an eye on its stability.

Apart from the use of concrete, another modern feature of the railway was the fact that the branch crossed the main line from the Up side by a flyover to avoid an express being impeded by the Lyme Regis train, or the branch train being delayed while waiting for a path across the main line.

The first train left Lyme Regis in rain on 24 August 1903 at 9.40 a.m., but by noon the sun had come out and hundreds of onlookers gathered at Lyme to watch the departure of the 12.25, a train of no less than thirteen coaches. Among its passengers were 200 children having a 'free' ride, the cost of which was defrayed by various people. On leaving with the dignitaries, the engine detonated fog signals.

The official party was entertained to a champagne buffet on the Down platform of Axminster station and then left at 1.18 for Lyme Regis where they lunched at the Royal Lion Hotel. Hitherto the horse bus had taken 50 minutes for the journey, but the train took only 25 minutes. The opening of the line caused the Cobb's remaining shipping to decline rapidly.

The branch flourished under the aegis of the LSWR and later the Southern Railway. It is recorded that 60,000 passengers, 10,000 parcels and 8,000 tons of goods travelled over the branch in 1908, the particularly heavy traffic probably due to the large numbers of sightseers who, during January to June of that year, came to view the burning cliff caused by natural deposits of bituminous shales and iron pyrites which had ignited spontaneously.

At first there were no fixed signals, and telephones were used to warn stations when trains were despatched. The Board of Trade insisted on a speed limit of 15 m.p.h. over Cannington Viaduct and the whole line was subject to a restriction of 25 m.p.h., reduced to 10 m.p.h. around curves of less than nine chains radius. In 1907 the LSWR took over the local company and generally upgraded the branch.

The first incursion of motor buses occurred in February 1920 when the Bridport–Charmouth–Axminster service caused the branch to lose much of its Charmouth traffic and by the summer of 1922 buses were operating between Lyme and Axminster.

When notice was given that the branch would close, residents of Combpyne claimed that with no bus service and with few car owners in the village, they would suffer. However, as only four tickets were issued at the station on an average winter's day, its retention could hardly be justified. Last trains ran on 29 November 1965. Passengers wishing to travel by the 3.39 p.m. ex-Lyme were unable to squeeze their way on to the platform. Civic parties from both ends of the line were on the train, some in period costume. The dignitaries attended a tea at Axminster, while the three-car DMU returned to Lyme to collect passengers who had been unable to board first time around. As stocks of day returns Lyme Regis–Axminster were exhausted, adults were issued with two children's returns. The final round trip left Axminster at 6.48 p.m. Lifting was completed by 28 June 1967, the contractor's diesel locomotive being C&M No. 22920 (Risley Yard No. 111 MED), built by John Fowler (Leeds) Limited in 1940.

In 1969 Minirail Ltd made a proposal to lay a 15 in gauge track from Combpyne station towards Axminster. The line was laid for 1¼ miles, but due to unfortunate difficulties with financial backing and with the Department of the Environment, the company went into liquidation and the track was lifted.

At Axminster station, 80 ft above sea-level, branch passenger trains used a new bay provided at the Down end of the Up main line platform, with a loop for the engine to run round the train, and a connection was put in between the Up siding and the bay line. There was no direct connection from the branch to the main line, a back shunt into a siding being necessary. A small coal stage was provided where the branch engine could be hand-coaled by the crew, and a water tank which took its supply from the River Axe. Trap points at the entrance to the bay protected passenger coaches from possible runaways.

Leaving the station, the line went westwards, rose on a gradient of 1 in 80 and curved to cross the main line by means of a girder flyover 17 ft 6 in in height. Until 5 September 1915 there was a trailing link connecting the branch with the Down sidings. The line climbed towards Combpyne at 1 in 40 and crossed the Fosse Way. Combpyne station, close to the summit of the line, was 470 ft above sea-level and had a crossing loop with an island platform until 1930 when the loop was converted to a siding. Quite divorced from the platform was a booking-office, shelter and retiring room for ladies. At one time the station name board read 'Combpyne for Landslip' and an extensive number of sightseers were handled to view the 1839 landslip between Lyme and Seaton. With the closure of the signal-box on 17 June 1930 the office of station-master was dispensed with and a leading porter under the control of the Lyme station-master appointed in his stead. Although the station closed to goods traffic on 5 December 1960, the siding was retained for stabling a camping coach. In 1955 the six-berth coach could be hired in the high season for a rental £9 per week. Both the coach and the station-house had water delivered daily by rail.

The line descended from a point a ¼ mile beyond Combpyne to Lyme Regis on a gradient of 1 in 40/73. Cannington viaduct had its piers constructed in 6 ft lifts, decreasing in length by 6 in and in width by 3 in. Its approximate cost was £9,100.

The inhabitants of Uplyme sent several petitions to the LSWR for a halt to be built near the New Inn. Eventually this was agreed, but before any action could be taken, the introduction of a motor bus service solved the problem. The line crossed the county boundary into Dorset just before passing under the A3070 prior to entering Lyme Regis.

As was generally the custom with small railways, the Axminster & Lyme Regis Light Railway did not purchase its own locomotive and rolling stock, but was worked by a larger company, in this case the LSWR, for 55 per cent of the gross receipts. As there was no suitable class of LSWR locomotive, it purchased two 0–6–0T 'Terriers' from the London, Brighton & South Coast Railway, No. 668 *Clapham* and No. 646 *Newington*, for £500 apiece. Repainted and numbered 734 and 735 respectively, they proved insufficiently powerful for the heavy summer traffic and the sharp curves caused them to suffer extensive tyre wear. In August 1905 an Adams 02 class 0–4–4T assisted, but because of the line's severe weight restrictions, the tanks and bunker could only be partly filled, which decreased the engine's usefulness. No. 228 had its side tanks marked to indicate the maximum permissible volume of water. In May 1907 the 'Terriers' departed for good. No. 734 was sold to the Freshwater, Yarmouth & Newport Railway in 1913. On Grouping in 1923 it became SR No. W2 and was named *Freshwater* in 1928, becoming No. W8 *Freshwater* in 1932. In 1949 it returned to the mainland as BR No. 32646 and principally worked on the Hayling Island service until closure, when it was stationed at Droxford and used on part of the Meon Valley line. Brickwood's brewery bought it in May 1966 and, restored as LBSCR No. 46 *Newington*, she was placed outside their inn, The Hayling Billy. The engine now works on the Isle of Wight Steam Railway. No. 735 was used on the Lee-on-Solent Light Railway and from 1930 until its withdrawal in 1936, acted as Carriage & Wagon Works pilot at Ashford.

The 02 class engines which took over the Lyme Regis branch did not prove to be really satisfactory, suffering from excessive flange wear and distorted frames. In 1913, therefore, Urie took Adams 415 class 4–4–2T No. 0125, built in 1885, and modified the bogie to give greater side play and thereby ease the negotiation of the severe curves with which the branch abounded. The alteration proved successful and was performed on two more engines. One was sub-shedded at Lyme Regis, while the other two were at the main shed, Exmouth Junction, either undergoing servicing, or operating on other lines, usually the Exmouth branch.

By November 1958 these engines were becoming aged and it was decided to try Western Region 0–4–2T No. 1462, locomotives of this class becoming available because of the introduction of DMUs on lines elsewhere. However, these engines had too long a wheelbase for the sharp curves and lost time on each trip through their inability to sustain the steaming rate required to climb the bank. In spite of this, engines of this class were used in times of motive power shortage.

Following extensive track renewals and re-aligning of curves early in 1960, an ex-LMS Ivatt Class 2 2–6–2T No. 41297 was tested. It proved successful and the civil engineer approved the use of this type in an emergency. The last 4–4–2T was condemned in July 1961 and the Class 2s were approved for general use. The Bluebell Railway purchased 4–4–2T No. 30583, while the other two were scrapped.

On 4 November 1963 a single-car DMU took over the branch working, though at busy times a three-car unit was used. Steam still made an occasional appearance.

With the opening of the line, six mixed trains were run in each direction taking 25 minutes each way for the distance of 6¾ miles. No trains were run on Sundays. By the summer of 1914 the service consisted of:

Down:	6 passenger;	3 mixed;	1 conditional goods
Up:	8 passenger;	1 mixed;	1 conditional goods

Passenger trains were scheduled to take 20 minutes. By 1963 trains were taking only 18 minutes in each direction, the Class 2 engines permitting a speedier journey. In 1965 an Indian Summer service was put on with twelve trains each way on Mondays to Fridays, including an evening through working to Exeter Central.

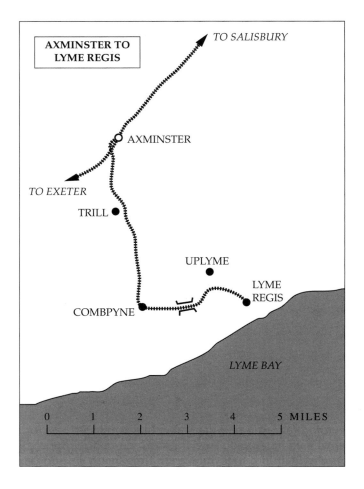

A horse bus stands outside Axminster station. Notice the unusually tall chimney stacks.

c. 1905 Author's collection

0415 class 4–4–2T No. 3520 (later BR No. 30584) standing in the Lyme Regis branch platform at Axminster. On the left can be seen the water tank, the chimney for the pumping engine's boiler, a sleeper-built coal stage and a water crane. The driver stands beside his engine.

c. 1932 Lens of Sutton

0415 class 4–4–2T No. 3520 standing in the bay platform at Axminster with a train for Lyme Regis. Note that the fishplates have been oiled to prevent the bolts rusting.

27.7.46 Pursey Short

Ivatt Class 2 2–6–2T No. 41307 at Axminster. An engine at the far end is shunting goods wagons.

c. 1960 Lens of Sutton

0415 class 4–4–2T No. 30583 shunting a through Lyme Regis to Waterloo coach on to an Up express at Axminster. Branch coach Set No. 101 stands in the bay platform. Notice the banner repeater signal to the left of the chimney.

18.7.58 P.Q. Treloar

4–4–2T No. 30583 on the sinuous line between Combpyne and Axminster.

18.7.58 P.Q. Treloar

Combpyne, view Up. A camping coach stands in the siding which until 12 August 1921 was a loop. Notice the water containers for the station-house.

c. 1960 Lens of Sutton

Constructing Cannington Viaduct. Notice the overhead pulley.

c. 1902 Author's collection

Cannington Viaduct – most of the walls have been built and a crane is at work. Centreing has not yet been removed from the three westernmost arches.

c. 1903 M.J. Tozer collection

Ivatt Class 2 2–6–2T No. 41206 (left) and No. 41291 (right) crossing Cannington Viaduct with the Locomotive Club of Great Britain's East Devon Tour. Notice the jack arch.

7.3.65 Hugh Ballantyne

Coaches on the 15 in gauge railway at Combpyne which Minirail Ltd had hoped to run.

3.6.76 Author

Seaton Junction to Seaton

Seaton was another town which the railway changed from port to resort. The plans for a line to Seaton were unusual in that they included a road bridge across the River Axe. The Seaton & Beer Railway Act was passed on 13 July 1863. The company's engineer was William Robert Galbraith, who held the same post in the LSWR which was to work the line. On 8 January 1864 a contract was signed with Howard Ashton Holden, London, for constructing the line. Little progress was made, Holden lacking the necessary finance, so the contract had to be terminated on 27 September 1865. John Sampson signed a contract on 10 October 1865 but he, too, was lacking funds. With three-quarters of the work still to be completed, a contract was signed with William Shrimpton on 17 February 1866, but then Holden threatened proceedings if Shrimpton started work. Sampson meanwhile continued. By August 1866 the bulk of the earthworks was completed and the line inspected by the Board of Trade on 27 December 1867. Colonel Yolland criticized a number of things and a second inspection was carried out on 2 March 1868. The line opened on 16 March but, unusually for the period, there were no public celebrations,

The road bridge connecting Seaton with Axmouth was not opened until 24 April 1877. This bridge, which still stands, is unusual in that the whole of the bridge and toll-house are of concrete; the house is reputed to be the oldest concrete house in England.

The Seaton & Beer Railway was taken over by the LSWR on 3 January 1888. The line was well used by holiday-makers. For instance, in August 1959 3,500 tickets were issued and 12,000 collected, while even in 1964 about 1,200 passengers used the station each Saturday in summer. However, Seaton and Colyton Town closed to goods on 3 February 1964 and passenger traffic was withdrawn on 7 March 1966 with less than a dozen passengers making the final trip.

With the opening of the branch, Colyton for Seaton was renamed Colyton Junction, changing to Seaton Junction in July 1869. The station was rebuilt with central through roads and platform loops in 1928. The branch junction faced Exeter and from the platform the line descended at a gradient of 1 in 100, steepening to 1 in 76 before Colyton Town, the suffix being dropped in September 1890. On the east side of the line stands the single platform with its station building vaguely Italianate in design, of red brick with bandings of yellow and black.

Leaving the station the line fell at 1 in 76/168; the length of about ¼ mile at 1 in 168 was curious in that the gradient posts at both ends pointed upwards! Colyford was a simple platform on the west side of the line, devoid of any sidings or goods facilities. At times when the the level-crossing was unmanned, the guard was responsible for working the gates.

Between Colyford and Seaton the line followed the estuary of the River Axe. Seaton, 4½ miles from the junction, had a terminal platform with two faces. In 1936 the Italianate

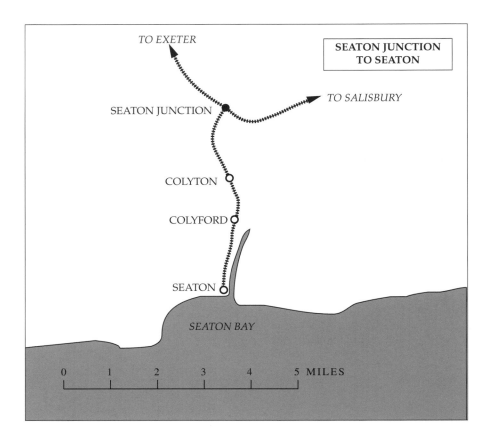

building was replaced with a modern concrete and brick structure. When in the early years of this century it was an 'open' station, a ticket platform was sited outside Seaton and working timetables carried a note that 'All Down passenger trains must stop at the ticket platform during the months June–September for the collection of tickets'.

In the 1860s Tartar class 2–2–2WTs No. 12 *Jupiter* and No. 33 *Phoenix* worked the branch and twenty years later Ilfracombe Goods 0–6–0s No. 282 and No. 284 regularly headed trains. Around the turn of the century 02 class 0–4–4Ts appeared and were the mainstay for many years. In the mid-twenties No. 183 and No. 236 of this class were motor-fitted and worked a push and pull train, but this mechanical form proved dangerous and was banned. They were replaced by an ex-LBSCR D1 class 0–4–2T No. B234 fitted for air control push and pull operation. This proved successful and as a consequence, several 02s and M7s were fitted with compressed air gear. They could be identified by a pump attached to the left-hand side of the smokebox and a reservoir immediately below the running plate. Spare Lyme Regis branch 4–4–2Ts appeared and 4–4–0s worked excursions. On 2 May 1963 M7 No. 30048 and a three-coach motor set worked the branch for the last time and working was taken over by WR 0–6–0PT No. 6400 and two auto-cars, the WR having assumed control of the line on 1 January 1963. On 4 November 1963 the branch was dieselized.

The timber engine shed at Seaton, costing £200, was replaced by a concrete block structure opened in 1936. The staff consisted of a shedman, two drivers and two firemen. Dieselization caused the shed to be closed on 4 November 1963. The severe winter of

1962/3 brought problems, the low temperatures causing the water column at Seaton to freeze. As the timetable did not permit a locomotive to run to Axminster where the nearest supply could be obtained, Exmouth Junction shed sent a Pacific to work services until the branch M7 was refilled by hose-pipe from the toilet at Seaton station. After an hour it had sufficient water to reach Axminster, but the Pacific remained for two days, working some of the trains.

The closure and lifting of the Seaton branch was not the end of rail transport along the valley. Modern Electric Tramways Limited, which had operated narrow gauge double-decker tramcars at Eastbourne since the 1950s, had been seeking a new location and eventually laid a 2 ft 9 in gauge line from Seaton to Colyton, the length to Seaton Junction having no traffic potential as Seaton Junction station had been closed.

The Seaton & District Electric Tramway Company opened to Bobsworth Bridge (so called as the return fare was 1s) on 28 August 1970. As the overhead was incomplete, power was obtained from a battery trailer. The line was extended to the south of the level-crossing at Colyford on 9 April 1971 and power from the overhead was first used on 23 September 1973. On 17 May 1975 an extension was opened to a more central terminus at the car park, Harbour Road. The extension to Colyton was opened on 8 March 1980.

The increased number of visitors to Colyton caused certain problems, and in 1980 the *Seaton News*, in connection with a parish council meeting at Colyton, reported: 'The council should write back to say the tram company should provide toilets and also point out that the flow of passengers was not seasonal . . . but all the year round'.

The 1930s style architecture of the exterior of Seaton station. A poster advertises cheap day returns to Exeter Central for 4s.

21.7.49 Pursey Short

Fleet list of rolling stock on the Seaton Tramway:

Works vehicles

No.	Date built	Type	Other information
01	1954	Mobile shop	
02	1969	Works car	
03	1986	Bogie wagon	
04	1987	Hoist wagon	
05	1988	Four-wheel wagon	
–		Side tipper wagon	
–	1959	Ruston & Hornsby four-wheel diesel locomotive, maker's No. 435398	Purchased from North Devon Clay Co. Ltd, Peters Marland, North Devon

Passenger-carrying stock

No.	Date built	No. of seats	Type
2	1964	35	Open top double-decker
4	1961	20	Blackpool 'Boat' single-decker
6	1955	37	Open top double-decker
7	1958	37	Open top double-decker
8	1968	41	Open top double-decker
12	1966	50	Open top double-decker
14	1904	27	Ex-Metropolitan Electric Tramways double-decker No. 94, rebuilt as single-decker 1969 and narrowed in width by a foot
16	1921	26	Ex-Bournemouth Corporation Tramways double-decker No. 106, rebuilt as a single-decker and narrowed to 5 ft 6 in
17	1988	48	Toast-rack. Seats lift out so that it can carry 10–12 passengers in wheelchairs, plus 8 helpers

02 class 0–4–4T No. 183 drifts into Seaton Junction, the through Seaton to Waterloo coach leading. This will be shunted to the rear of the Up train, whose engine may be seen above the left-hand bill hoarding.

29.5.36 S.W. Baker

A Gloucestershire Railway Carriage & Wagon Company single-car DMU stands at the branch platform, Seaton Junction.

1964 Lens of Sutton

K10 class 4–4–0 No. 384 and nine six-wheel coaches approach Seaton Junction with a returning Bank Holiday excursion.

6.8.34 S.W. Baker

Motor set No. 381 leaves Colyton working the 2.05 p.m. Seaton Junction to Seaton, M7 class 0–4–4T No. 30021 propelling.

2.6.59 J.H. Aston

M7 class 0–4–4T No. 30048 with an Up train pauses at Colyton to attach or detach a van.

c. 1960 Lens of Sutton

Ex-GWR 64XX class 0–6–0PT No. 6412 works the 2.20 p.m. Seaton to Seaton Junction service. Notice the water tank at the far end of the platform. No. 6412 is preserved on the West Somerset Railway.

26.10.63 E. Wilmshurst

BR Standard Class 3 2–6–2T No. 82040 at Colyton with a Seaton Junction to Seaton train, substituting for a DMU. Unusually no disc or headlamp is carried. A loading gauge stands above the site of a siding, the yard having been taken out of use on 19 May 1964. Lifted track components can be seen.

26.9.64 A.E. West

Ex-GWR 64XX class 0–6–0PT No. 6400 near Colyford working the 11.53 a.m. ex-Seaton Junction hauling WR auto-trailers.

24.8.63 Author

Gloucester Railway Carriage & Wagon Company single-car DMU approaches the level-crossing north of Colyford station on a Down working.

1964 Lens of Sutton

Ex-LBSCR D1 class 0–4–2T No. B214 beside the water tank at Seaton. The coaches are the 1914 'gated' stock, probably Set No. 373. To the left of the locomotive's chimney is the water tank gauge. The pointer stands near the base of the scale indicating a full tank.

c. 1931 Lens of Sutton

A view north during reconstruction of the platform at Seaton which is being widened and lengthened. Notice the upturned loading gauge. S11 class 4–4–0 No. 399 is being watered. The old engine shed has been removed, but not yet replaced.

1.6.36 S.W. Baker

02 class 0–4–4T No. 187 about to leave Seaton. Notice the apparatus on the engine for air-controlled motor train operation. The concrete River Axe road bridge is on the left.

5.8.33 S.W. Baker

Car No. 8 bound for Seaton leaves Colyford.

3.6.76 Author

Sidmouth Junction to Sidmouth

The first railway at Sidmouth was an independent line. It carried stone, used to construct two jetties, from Hook Ebb, a reef situated 1¾ miles to the east. In order to prevent part of the line being swept away by a storm, a tunnel was cut through Salcombe Hill. One third of a mile in length, it ran parallel with the cliff face and only a few feet from it. In 1837 a steam locomotive was delivered by sea to Exmouth and drawn by horses to Sidmouth. Unfortunately it proved to be too large for the tunnel, but in order not to waste such an attraction, it was coupled to wagons and for a small sum passengers were carried along the Esplanade for pure entertainment. The jetty project was abandoned and the engine removed by the following year.

On 7 August 1862 the Sidmouth Railway & Harbour Company's Act was passed, but the scheme proved unpopular and subscriptions were slow – not surprising as some trickery had been perpetrated. Shareholders had been divided into two classes: Class A, which included Sidmouth residents, and Class B, which comprised those in London. Calls for money were only made on Class A. The company was wound up in 1869.

The Act for buildings the 8¼ mile long Sidmouth Railway was passed on 29 June 1871. The following year the tender of R.T. Relf, Okehampton, was accepted. The line as laid was single, but sufficient land was purchased to allow doubling. The branch opened on 6 July 1874, only a week late.

The first train left Sidmouth Junction at 6.50 a.m. on 6 July. No official opening ceremony was held that day, but 200 people gathered to see the inaugural train leave. Rather unusually, celebrations were spread out over no less than four days. On the first day 800 children marched behind a band from the Esplanade to Sidmouth station to watch the departure of the 2.45 p.m. and cheered 'loudly and long'. They then adjourned to a nearby field for tea and games. Tipton and Ottery also celebrated by holding teas for the young and old. The following day a dinner at Sidmouth Town Hall was held for railway shareholders, officials, gentry and tradesmen.

Regatta day was on 8 July and because of the railway more people attended, one special train of seventeen coaches being double-headed. *Lethaby's Sidmouth Journal & Directory* reported: 'There was a seeming incongruity in linking the railway opening with a waterside rollicking; and in providing an amusement which is proverbial for bringing together all the rowdyism of a district . . . giving knaves a welcome and thereby attracting the fools on whom such knaves flourish'. Select Sidmouth was experiencing just the sort of behaviour it feared would occur when the branch was opened.

On 9 July a public dinner for 400 elderly people was held, sixpence being given to those under seventy and a shilling to those above that age. Eighty-one 'very aged and infirm' folk who were unable to attend received half a crown each, while 84 lb of surplus meat and 24 lb of plum pudding was divided among thirty families.

The line proved successful in financial terms and in 1894 the working company, the LSWR, attempted to purchase it, but the line remained independent until 1922. When the 1963 Beeching Report threatened the line with closure, the town's hoteliers and shopkeepers, anxious to keep the line open, formed the Sidmouth Railway Committee. About 120 people attended its first meeting. In 1964 20 per cent of visitors still used rail transport. Some 900 passengers used Sidmouth station on a summer Saturday and 30 to 40 daily in winter, the number increasing to over 100 in summer. The annual total was 175,000 and Tipton and Ottery St Mary together accounted for a further 115,000.

The committee's efforts, however, were in vain. The last train on the branch was the 18.57 Sidmouth Junction to Sidmouth on 6 March 1967. Withdrawal of services meant that Tipton was no longer the West Country's last junction between two single line branches. Even just prior to closure it was served by almost thirty trains daily.

The two-platformed Sidmouth Junction experienced an exceptional number of name changes. Opened as Feniton on 18 July 1860, it became Ottery & Sidmouth Road on 1 July 1861; Feniton for Ottery St Mary in February 1868; Ottery Road in April 1868; Sidmouth Junction on 6 July 1874 and reverted to Feniton when reopened on 3 May 1971. It had been closed concurrently with the Sidmouth branch.

Sidmouth trains used the bay platform at the east end of the Down platform, trains entering it facing Exeter. As no engine release road was provided, a train had to be backed out in order for the locomotive to run round, but the entire movement could be performed without fouling the main line.

On leaving the junction the branch descended a gradient of 1 in 110 soon steepening to 1 in 53, but subsequently had easy gradients along the valley of the River Otter to Ottery St Mary. Here was a typical country station with crossing loop, three sidings and a goods shed. Like all the stations on the branch, it was built of brick.

Tipton St John's, merely Tipton until 1 February 1881, was a busy two-platform station immediately north of the junction of the Exmouth and Sidmouth branches and was equipped with locomotive watering facilities. Camping coaches were stabled in one of the three sidings.

From Tipton the Sidmouth branch rose at 1 in 45 for 2 miles to Bowd Summit in Harpford Woods, and then fell for about 1 mile at 1 in 54 to the terminus 200 ft above sea-level and ¾ mile from the beach. It was said that the inland site was to discourage trippers spoiling the select town. The station building had Italianate features and its single platform held seven coaches on one side and five on the other. This limited accommodation caused problems on occasions, such as when the 'City of Plymouth Holiday Express' arrived with nine coaches; another engine had to shunt the rear coaches to the other platform face.

Probably the first class of engine to work the branch was a Beattie 2–4–0WT. Adams 02 class 0–4–4Ts made their appearance around 1890 and in the 1930s several members of this class were fitted with compressed air gear for working push and pull trains, but the larger M7 0–4–4Ts gradually ousted them. In the BR period, ex-LMS and BR Standard Class 2MT 2–6–2Ts appeared, BR Standard Class 3MT 2–6–2Ts and BR Standard Class 4MT 2–6–4Ts.

West Country class 4–6–2 No. 21C110 *Sidmouth* traversed the branch on 27 June 1946 for its naming ceremony, but normally engines of this type never used the line. Guests at the naming ceremony were entertained to tea in a restaurant car. By the time 21C145 *Ottery St Mary* was named, enthusiasm for these ceremonies had waned!

The branch was dieselized on 4 November 1963 using DMUs. These were restricted to a maximum speed of 50 m.p.h. between Sidmouth Junction and Tipton and 40 m.p.h. between there and Sidmouth.

At 1.30 a.m. on Sunday 7 January 1900 the small timber engine shed at Sidmouth was

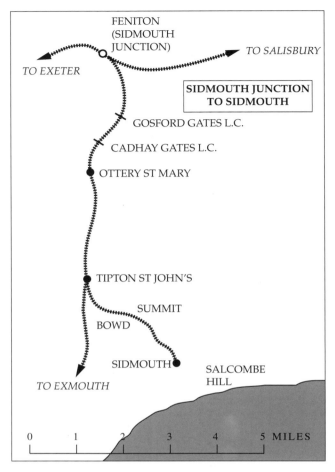

found to be blazing. Falkner, the station-master living in the nearby station-house, promptly summoned his staff and they worked hard to douse the flames. It was a hopeless task. A gale spread the fire so quickly that the shed was completely destroyed. Inside the blazing shed, 02 0–4–4T No. 195 had its paintwork burnt off. The shed was rebuilt, but closed a few years before the Second World War.

When the branch opened in 1874, seven passenger trains ran each way daily, taking 28 to 30 minutes in each direction. No Sunday service was run. In the summer of 1914 eleven passenger trains ran each way, some doing the journey in 23 minutes. One goods train was run in each direction, the working timetable stipulating that a 'heavy brake van' should be at the rear. There was also one Down mixed train. The 1938 summer timetable showed twenty-four trains each way on Mondays to Fridays operating over all, or part of, the branch, while on Saturdays there were thirty Down and twenty-eight Up workings. On Sundays eleven Down and twelve Up trains ran and there was also one each way between Sidmouth and Exmouth.

The DMU service in the summer of 1964, a journey which took about 21 minutes, showed eleven Down and ten Up trains Mondays to Fridays, plus one each way between Sidmouth and Exmouth. On Saturdays this increased to nineteen Down and twenty-one Up, including two each way between Sidmouth and Exmouth. The Sunday service was ten in each direction.

Poster, 1912.

Ivatt Class 2 2–6–2T No. 41318 of 72A stands in the Down bay with the 10.55 a.m. to Sidmouth, while 'Merchant Navy' class No. 35025 *Brocklebank Line*, working the 8.10 a.m. Ilfracombe to Waterloo, picks up through coaches from the 9.52 a.m. Exmouth and 10.20 Sidmouth. No. 35025 is now preserved.

31.5.63 J.H. Aston

Triple-headed trains were rare in England. BR Standard Class 3 2–6–2T No. 82018 and No. 82010 and Ivatt Class 2 3–6–2T No. 41318 leave Sidmouth Junction with a train from Cleethorpes consisting of four Eastern Region coaches for Sidmouth and six for Exmouth.

30.7.60 S.P. Derek

Ground frame at Cadhay Gates. Notice the platform for unloading the water supply for the lodge.
6.10.64 South Western Circle Wessex Collection

Pullman Holiday Coach No. P48 at Tipton St John's.

8.9.61 South Western Circle Wessex Collection

M7 class 0–4–4T No. 30323 with the 2.04 p.m. Sidmouth Junction to Sidmouth crosses an Up train at Tipton St John's.

3.7.56 Hugh Ballantyne

BR Standard Class 2 2–6–2T No. 84020 leaves Tipton St John's for Sidmouth.

20.9.61 South Western Circle Wessex Collection

The 5.51 p.m. Tipton St John's to Exmouth, right, and the 5.42 p.m. Sidmouth to Sidmouth Junction cross at Tipton.

9.5.64 Author

A Birmingham Railway Carriage & Wagon Company DMU, the leading car of which is No. W51329, had descended the bank and arrives at Tipton St John's working the 5.42 p.m. Sidmouth to Sidmouth Junction. The branch to Budleigh Salterton is on the right. The '9A' is a bridge number plate.

9.5.64 Author

Ivatt Class 2 2–6–2T No. 41323 (72A) with the 10.28 a.m. Sidmouth Junction to Sidmouth north of the terminus.

24.8.63 Author

Exterior of Sidmouth station. Notice the canopy sheltering the entrance so that in wet weather intending passengers could step dry shod from carriage or bus. The rear of the engine shed can be seen on the left.

c. 1905 Author's collection

T1 class 0–4–4T (probably No. 76) arriving at Sidmouth.

c. 1910 Author's collection

T1 class 0–4–4T No. 14 at Sidmouth.

c. 1928 Freda Clayton

A BR Standard 2–6–2T runs round its train following arrival at Sidmouth.

c. 1958 M.E.J. Deane

Tipton St John's to Exmouth

After several abortive attempts to build a line to Budleigh Salterton, a successful scheme was proposed by the Budleigh Salterton Railway. Its Act was passed on 20 July 1894, enabling a line to be built from the Sidmouth branch at Tipton.

The first sod was cut at Greenway Lane, Budleigh Salterton, by Lady Gertrude Rolle, wife of the owner of most of the land through which the line was to pass. Lucas & Aird were the contractors and they completed the line six months ahead of time – quite an achievement as most lines opened later than planned.

On 14 May 1897 Mrs Hugh Williams-Drummond, daughter of the Hon. Mark Rolle and wife of the company's chairman, 'drove' the inaugural train headed by No. 359, a T1 class 0–4–4T decorated with flags, evergreens and her portrait. At Tipton the village schoolmaster conducted his pupils singing the National Anthem and the train exploded detonators as it left the station and started on the new branch. Unfortunately Mrs Williams-Drummond overran Budleigh station and had to set back. The train was welcomed at Salterton by the strains of the Sidmouth Volunteers' Band and by civic officials. Mrs Williams-Drummond declared the line open and her husband formally handed it over to the LSWR, the working company; luncheon followed. The day was a public holiday and many of the streets and houses were decorated. A free tea was provided for children under fourteen. The LSWR absorbed the company on 1 January 1912.

The LSWR Act of 25 July 1898 authorized the construction of the Exmouth & Salterton Railway. The work began in 1899, the *South Western Gazette* commenting: 'No Royal Presence, no Duke or Duchess with silver spade, no Director, not even an officer of the company, but only an office boy out of bounds witnessed the cutting of the first sod on one of the prettiest five miles of railway in the sunny south'. The contractor was Henry Lovatt & Sons, who had also built sections of the Manchester Ship Canal and the Great Central Railway.

The branch was very expensive to construct, one of the costly works being a lengthy 30 ft high viaduct near Exmouth. Another expensive work was Knowle cutting, and the excavated soil from here was tipped on the foreshore near Exmouth station. It quickly built up to road level and provided the site on which a new goods depot was subsequently built. Hundreds of navvies were needed for the line's construction and a mission was set up in the King's Cinema, Exeter Road, Exmouth, which had just been converted from the abandoned St Margaret's Church. Later it became the Royal Cinema.

The line opened on Whit Monday 1 June 1903. The first train, four coaches in length, left Exmouth at 6.58 a.m. and so great was the demand that a duplicate had to be run. With dignitaries aboard, the train left at 10.40 and returned from Salterton at noon, its passengers then attending a luncheon. Every train on the line was well filled. The Rolle

Hotel horse bus, hitherto the only passenger conveyance between Exmouth and Salterton, was now superfluous. In winter it cost 9*d* to travel in comparative warmth inside and 6*d* to brave the elements on top, while in summer one suffocated inside for 6*d*, or enjoyed the fresh air on top for 9*d*.

With the development of road transport after the Second World War the line became uneconomic and made an annual loss of £21,000. The Minister of Transport consented to the line's closure on condition that certain road improvements were carried out and in due course passenger trains were withdrawn on 6 March 1967. Track recovery commenced on 28 May 1968, a Type 2 North British diesel-hydraulic locomotive of the D63XX series hauling a train of 16 open wagons, 2 bogie bolsters and 2 brake vans. Work finished in September.

From Tipton St John's the line fell at 1 in 150, crossed the River Otter and descended at 1 in 360 to Newton Poppleford. Opened on 1 June 1899, the station, built of brick with part of its roof forming the platform awning, was situated on the Down side of the single line. Placed at the foot of the hill at the east end of the village it also served Harpford across the river. The station, closed to goods from 27 January 1964, dealt with fruit and flower traffic in addition to general goods. The line crossed the River Otter twice more and reached Colaton Raleigh siding, in use until 1 February 1953.

East Budleigh was simply Budleigh until 27 April 1898. The brick-built station building, still in existence as a private house, stood on the Up side of the single line. A large awning sheltered the platform, on which also stood a small brick goods shed.

The line fell, then rose at 1 in 50 from the Otter valley to Budleigh Salterton, just Salterton until 27 April 1898. The two-road station of brick was built by J.C. Palmer, a local builder, for £350. He also constructed Budleigh station.

About 1919, during the herring season, as many as four vans of fish for Billingsgate Market would be attached to an afternoon passenger train. From 1939 shellfish were sent in small barrels. Arriving by rail from Kingsbridge in large barrels, they were sorted at Budleigh. In the 1950s up to 40,000 tons of stone containing silica were despatched annually to Albright & Wilson, Portishead. It also dealt with coal for the gas works and, after the market which was held on alternate Mondays, twenty to twenty-five cattle trucks would usually require loading. Budleigh Salterton closed to goods traffic on 27 January 1964.

The single needle telegraph was still in use at Budleigh Salterton in 1919. In the interests of brevity code words were used. Two of these were 'Gum' and 'Falcon', the first meaning 'Referring to your communication of today' and the second 'No trace'. One day the junior porter was standing on the platform talking to a clergyman when the signalman, having received a telegraph message from Tipton St John's box, came out of his cabin and called to inquire if an article of lost property had been handed out from the previous Down train. The clerk, busy dealing with parcels on the platform shouted back, 'Give the b——s the Gum Falcon', whereupon the clergyman remarked, 'I understand the first part, but what does he mean by "Gum Falcon"?'

Trains continued climbing at 1 in 50 for 1½ miles to the summit at Knowle cutting and then descended on the same gradient to Littleham. The brick-built station building with awning was on the Up platform, while the Down had a small timber waiting shelter. Following the housing development which occurred after the Second World War, it was not unusual for twenty women, some with prams, to be waiting for a train to Exmouth. Between two and four camping coaches were kept in the yard.

The line descended at 1 in 50 and, approaching the junction with the line from Exmouth Junction, crossed the major engineering feature, a curved 370 yd long, 30 ft high brick-built viaduct of twenty-three arches, wide enough for double track.

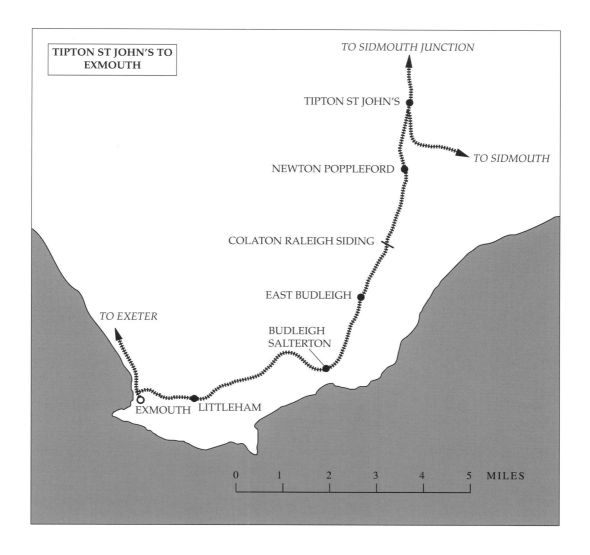

TIPTON ST JOHN'S TO EXMOUTH

TO SIDMOUTH JUNCTION

TIPTON ST JOHN'S

TO SIDMOUTH

NEWTON POPPLEFORD

COLATON RALEIGH SIDING

EAST BUDLEIGH

BUDLEIGH SALTERTON

TO EXETER

EXMOUTH   LITTLEHAM

| 0 | 1 | 2 | 3 | 4 | 5 | MILES |

The 11 mile long line was worked by the same types of locomotive as worked the Sidmouth branch. A small wooden engine shed was in use when the line opened, but was rendered redundant on the opening of the extension to Exmouth.

The first train service on 15 May 1897 gave eight trains each way on weekdays only between Tipton St John's and Budleigh Salterton. The summer of 1932 saw thirteen trains each way on Mondays to Fridays, two of which were through, to or from Sidmouth in each direction. On Saturdays there was an additional Up train and instead of through trains to Sidmouth, five Up and eight Down had coaches running to or from Sidmouth Junction. On Sundays six ran each way with one Down train each from Sidmouth, Sidmouth Junction and Ottery St Mary. No Sunday service was run in the winter.

With the commencement of the summer 1966 timetable, through workings to and from Exeter via Exmouth ceased in order to facilitate closure at a date then unannounced. A reduced service of eight trains ran each way. On summer Saturdays ten trains ran each way. The final weekday service consisted of seven trains.

A DMU arrives at Newton Poppleford with an Exmouth to Sidmouth train on the final day of working.

4.3.67 R.A. Lumber

M7 class 0–4–4T No. 30670 leaves Budleigh Salterton for Sidmouth Junction.

8.9.61 South Western Circle Wessex Collection

02 class 0–4–4T No. 203 arrives at Budleigh Salterton with a Down train.

c. 1930 M.E.J. Deane

The recently completed Knowle cutting before the slopes had time to be grassed.

1903 Author's collection

ER stock of the first Cleethorpes to Exmouth train being berthed at Littleham on 18 June 1960 by BR Standard Class 3 2–6–2T No. 82010. This was uneconomic use of the stock as it remained idle until the following Saturday.

18.6.60 S.P. Derek

Ex-US Army motor lorry engaged at Budleigh Salterton on track recovery.

20.7.68 R.A. Lumber

415 class 4–4–2T No. 82 at Littleham with an Exmouth train.

c. 1905 Author's collection

Littleham station.

c. 1903 Author's collection

Exmouth Junction to Exmouth

The Exeter & Exmouth Railway Company's Act was passed on 2 July 1855 and the ceremony of turning the first sod took place on 27 November 1856 at the site of Exmouth station, where events were far from auspicious. It was a day of dual festivities as it coincided with the celebration of the 21st birthday of the Hon. Mark Rolle. He was 2 hours late arriving for the ceremony of turning the turf. Presumably famished, he then alighted as the directors' carriage passed the Market House where the feast was to be held after the ceremony, leaving the honours to be performed by the chairman, John Walker. In lifting the turf, Walker broke the spade handle and completed the task with his hands. The Exeter & Exmouth was to have been a broad gauge line, but in September 1857 the standard gauge Yeovil & Exeter Railway resolved to build from its main line a branch to Topsham leaving the Exeter & Exmouth to complete the remainder also on the standard gauge. This change was authorized in a new Act of 28 June 1858, the LSWR receiving powers to make the branch to Topsham on 12 July 1858.

By March 1859 a contract for the construction was signed with James Taylor of Exeter. He converted some of the clay excavated from cuttings into bricks for bridges and culverts. At 7.46 a.m. on 1 May 1861 the first train, consisting of eleven coaches and carrying about 150 passengers, left Exeter drawn by No. 36 *Comet*, a 2–2–2WT decorated with flags, to travel the completed 9½ mile long line. It arrived at Exmouth 30 minutes later. The second train arrived with 500 passengers in nineteen coaches behind two locomotives, and a third train, again piloted, consisted of sixteen coaches.

At 3.00 p.m. a banquet was held at the Globe Hotel, Exmouth, enlivened when a speaker advocating free trade was pelted with orange peel and a physical struggle broke out. During the first five days, the line was used by an average of more than 2,000 passengers daily and the number of tickets issued to 31 August 1861 was 80,000. The branch carried 159,416 passengers in its first six months, but despite its initial promise the company was amalgamated with the LSWR on 1 January 1866 because sufficient capital could not be raised.

With the completion of doubling the track between Exmouth Junction and Topsham on 1 June 1908, two intermediate halts were opened served by a new Exeter to Topsham steam railmotor. The line was almost completely dieselized on 9 September 1963. To avoid closure, economies were made: unstaffing arrangements were introduced on 28 February 1965 and buildings at Polsloe Bridge, Exton and Lympstone were subsequently boarded up. Passengers purchased their tickets from guards equipped with an Omniprinter ticket machine, the first to be used in the West Country. Early in 1969 all surplus track was lifted at Exmouth station, its booking-office and hall closed, leaving just one entrance to a ticket kiosk erected on the sole platform in use, and the station frontage was leased as shops. It was about this time that revenue stopped declining and began to 'hold'. A further economy was the singling of the Exmouth Junction to Topsham section in February 1973.

In 1974 the annual cost of the line was:

		£
Train costs		75,000
Terminal costs		22,000
Track & signalling costs		51,000
Administration costs		19,000
	Total	167,000

Receipts were only £71,000, the deficit of £96,000 being made up in the form of a grant from the Department of the Environment.

The planning of an urban relief road at Exmouth required the demolition of the station and a new terminus was built set back 80 yd from the existing one. It was designed to form part of a transport complex consisting of car park, bus and railway station, the £100,000 costs falling on Devon County Council. The first train into the station was the 13.56 on 2 May 1976. The following day Lympstone Commando station was opened specially to serve about 1,400 personnel in barracks at the Royal Marines Commando Training Centre. In December Topsham, Exton and Lympstone stations were improved at a cost of £15,000, shared equally by BR and the County Council. The work involved replacing some of the old buildings with modern passenger shelters and installing new lighting.

From the Salisbury to Exeter main line the branch falls at 1 in 100 to Polsloe Bridge halt opened on 1 June 1908. The line continues to fall at 1 in 100, becomes level and then rises at 1 in 100, decreasing to 1 in 400 as it climbs to the summit, before descending for 3¼ miles to beyond Topsham. A ½ mile bank at 1 in 120 ends at Clyst St Mary & Digby halt. It was closed on 27 September 1948 and the sleeper-built structure dismantled soon after. Situated on the north side of the bridge over the Exeter to Sidmouth road, it was used by the village, 1 mile distant, as well as serving Digby Mental Hospital. At the time of writing, a new station, Digby & Sowton, is to be built just to the south to serve an industrial estate and shopping complex.

Digby's siding trailed off the Up line, three or four coal wagons being detached every fortnight for the hospital. The siding closed on 10 January 1957 when its services were no longer required by the hospital.

The line steepens to 1 in 100 for a mile, and a short distance down the gradient were Newcourt sidings, its three roads laid by United States' forces on 24 October 1943. Latterly these sidings were used by the Ministry of Defence as a Naval Stores Depot; they closed early in 1986.

Topsham, the most important intermediate station on the branch, still has its double track retained to form a passing loop. The red brick station building on the Up platform, designed by Sir William Tite, received a cream rendering in SR days. Goods traffic ceased on 4 December 1967. Raspberries, cherries and plums were despatched by passenger train from Topsham, practically every train in the season carrying fruit. Locally caught salmon were sent from the station. A local nursery specializing in orchids despatched twenty to thirty consignments daily. The station had a lilac hedge and it was the custom that one evening, while the hedge was in flower, the staff returned, cut the blooms and sent them to Covent Garden. They donated the proceeds to the LSWR/SR Orphanage.

Topsham station was lit by gas until 1976. When the pipes were renewed in 1958 the redundant piping was used to strengthen the straight letters of 'Topsham' done in topiary, a feature of the station since 1947. The curved letters were supported by signalling and telegraph wire.

At the southern end of the station a branch thirty-two chains in length led down to the quay, its route now being Holman Way. When the Exeter & Exmouth was under construction, some of the earth excavated from cuttings was used to extend the quay 80 ft into the estuary. The LSWR made this investment because of the difficulty of establishing docks at Exmouth. The Topsham Quay line opened on 23 September 1861.

As the branch was on a gradient of 1 in 38, trains were restricted to the equivalent of eight loaded goods wagons; in wet weather four was the usual limit. Before reaching the catch points at the head of the gradient, the second guard was required to hold over the points. A special light brake van of open construction had always to be placed at the Quay end of the train; before its introduction, two porters were required to walk beside the trucks ready to thrust in sprags should this prove necessary. About 1924 five wagons ran into the river and had to be hauled back by a steam crane. The 02 class 0-4-4Ts were the largest locomotives permitted to work the line. Latterly it was worked thrice weekly until its closure in 1957.

Beyond Topsham the single line reaches the Exe estuary and follows the shore for the rest of the journey to Exmouth, crossing the 114 yd long five-span River Clyst Viaduct. A replacement viaduct, opened in December 1961, allowed heavier engines to work the line. Beyond this, Odam's siding, about 500 yd in length, trailed to a fertilizer factory. It was taken out of use on 25 February 1940.

As Woodbury Road was some 2 miles from the village, from 15 September 1958 the station was appropriately named Exton after the nearer hamlet. Its goods sidings, closed to traffic on 6 March 1961, were retained for two camping coaches until lifting on 19 February 1965.

Topiary on the Down platform at Topsham.

24.10.78 Author

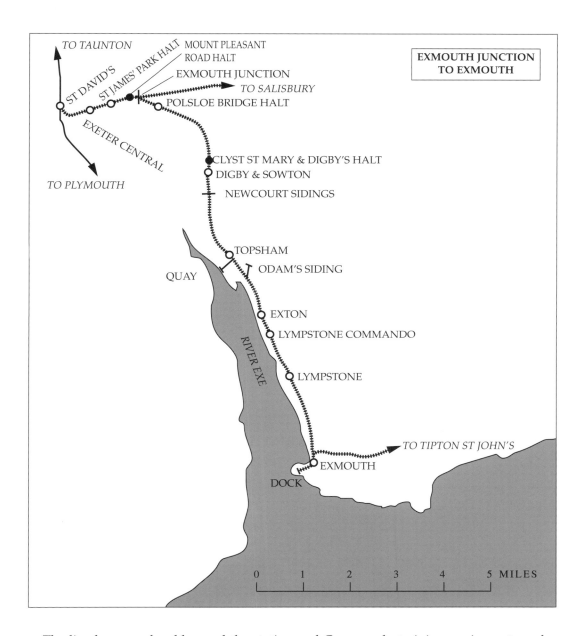

TO TAUNTON

ST JAMES' PARK HALT

MOUNT PLEASANT
ROAD HALT

EXMOUTH JUNCTION

ST DAVID'S

TO SALISBURY

POLSLOE BRIDGE HALT

EXETER CENTRAL

TO PLYMOUTH

CLYST ST MARY & DIGBY'S HALT

DIGBY & SOWTON

NEWCOURT SIDINGS

TOPSHAM

ODAM'S SIDING

QUAY

EXTON

LYMPSTONE COMMANDO

RIVER EXE

LYMPSTONE

TO TIPTON ST JOHN'S

EXMOUTH

DOCK

0   1   2   3   4   5 MILES

The line becomes level beyond the station and Commando training equipment can be seen on the left before the line reaches Lympstone Commando station, which serves the Royal Marines Centre exclusively.

The gradient then rises to 1 in 117 for just over ¼ mile before approaching Lympstone station. Goods facilities were withdrawn on 4 April 1960.

The original Exmouth station was two converted houses, but the extra traffic consequent upon the opening of the Budleigh Salterton line demanded an enlarged facility. This opened on 20 July 1924, the number of platforms being doubled to four. Following the closure of the Budleigh Salterton line, three platform roads were taken out of use on 20 December 1968 and on 2 May 1976 Exmouth's third station was open.

Exmouth Docks and branch line opened in 1868. Almost all traffic was inwards, much of it going by rail to branch stations. Apart from coal there was timber, wood pulp, grain and fertilizer, as well as cider apples and apple juice from France for Whiteway's, Whimple. The quay line closed on 10 March 1968, the same date as Exmouth goods yard.

The first locomotives on the Exmouth line were 2–2–2WTs and 2–4–0WTs, one of the latter being No. 298, later BR No. 30587 and now in the South Devon Railway's Museum at Buckfastleigh, while another was No. 314, later BR No. 35585, which can be seen at the Buckinghamshire Railway Centre, Quainton Road. From the 1880s Adams 415 class 4–4–2Ts worked the branch together with 02 class 0–4–4Ts. Drummond H13 class steam railcars Nos 5 and 6 were used for the service which began between Exeter and Topsham on 1 June 1908. M7 class 0–4–4Ts took over Exmouth services in the early forties and Ivatt Class 2 2–6–2Ts from July 1952, followed by BR Standard Class 2 and Class 3 2–6–2Ts. From June 1962 BR Standard Class 4 2–6–4Ts appeared.

The original timber built shed at Exmouth was replaced by a single road shed of concrete blocks opened in the late twenties. In 1960 it was allocated four engines. It had no coaling facilities, each engine visiting the parent shed at Exmouth Junction daily. The shed closed on 4 November 1963.

Today, although the branch is usually worked by DMUs, any locomotive hauled train required to or from Lympstone Commando is obliged to have an engine at both ends.

The opening service on the branch was five trains each way including Sundays, this being most unusual as branches generally had a less frequent service on Sundays, and often no trains at all. By 1887 ten Down and eleven Up trains were run, with five each way on Sundays. From 1 June 1908, as well as the eighteen trains each way Exeter to Exmouth and six on Sundays, a railmotor made an additional ten trips each way daily Exeter to Topsham and five on Sundays. With the demise of the railmotors, the Topsham shuttle service ceased.

The first SR summer timetable showed twenty Down and twenty-one Up trains. In the summer of 1948 there were twenty-three Down and twenty-four Up trains and thirteen each way on Sundays. The first DMU timetable for the winter of 1963/4 showed twenty-seven Down and twenty-nine Up trains, with eleven each way on Sundays. The following summer there were through workings to Saltash, Ilfracombe, Paignton, Barnstaple Junction and Tiverton. From May 1977 nearly all trains went through to Exeter, St David's, rather than terminating at Exeter Central. The summer timetable 1994 shows twenty-nine trains each way on weekdays, giving a half-hour frequency, with twenty-seven on Saturdays and thirteen on Sundays.

Arrival of a double-headed train on the opening day at Exmouth.
1.5.1861 Courtesy: *Illustrated London News*

M7 class 0–4–4T No. 377 arrives at Polsloe Bridge halt on an Exmouth to Exeter train. The platform is made of components cast at the nearby SR concrete depot.

May 1936 S.W. Baker

M7 class 0–4–4T No. 30671 arrives at Polsloe Bridge halt with an Exmouth to Exeter train.
22.8.50 South Western Circle Wessex Collection

Topsham, view in the Up direction.

c. 1905 Author's collection

Viewed from the window of a DMU to Exmouth, Set 827 leaves Topsham with the 10.30 Exmouth to Barnstaple.

19.7.89 Author

View of Lympstone Commando station from the cab of the DMU working the 10.27 Exeter, St David's to Exmouth.

19.7.89 Author

Down train hauled by an 02 class 0–4–4T arriving at Woodbury Road. The estuary of the River Exe is to the left.

c. 1910 Author's collection

A Down train hauled by an 02 class 0–4–4T north of Lympstone station.

c. 1910 Author' collection

DMU Set 871, comprising cars No. 53256 and No. 53639, working the 10.27 Exeter, St David's to Exmouth. The estuary of the River Exe is in the background. This photograph is taken from the same location as the one above, but from the opposite side of the road.

20.7.89 Author

Two-car DMU Set 861 (front) and 955 (rear) approaches Lympstone with the 17.09 Exeter, St David's to Exmouth.

20.7.89 Author

Signalman Frank Love changing the token at Lympstone with the fireman of an Up train.

c. 1925 Miss M.M. Love

Two-car DMU Set 957 working the 17.15 Exmouth to Exeter Central passing the Exmouth caution board.

21.7.89 Author

A train for Exeter Central leaving the four-platformed station at Exmouth.

c. 1955 M.E.J. Deane

DMU Set P463 comprising cars W51305, W59472 and W51320, arrives at Exmouth with the 08.26 from Exeter, St David's.

18.8.78 Author

An early view of Exmouth station.

c. 1865 Author's collection

Branch Lines from Tiverton Junction

The Culm Valley Light Railway Act was passed on 15 May 1873. Although work on the 7½ mile long line started early the following year, it proceeded too slowly for the engineer, Arthur C. Pain's liking. Some of the trouble was caused in June 1875 when the ballast engine bringing ballast from the pit at Craddock broke down, and some by the competition for labour from farmers at harvest time. The line was eventually finished in 1876, having taken double the anticipated time to construct, and Colonel Yolland made the Board of Trade inspection on 20 May.

On the opening day, 29 May 1876, there were grand ceremonies so beloved by the Victorians, while children and parents were given a free ride from Hemyock to Culmstock and back.

During the first six months of 1877 the line carried 19,949 passengers and 3,731 tons of goods and minerals, but two years later a trade recession caused figures to drop and the company suffered a cash shortage so severe, in fact, that small parcels of land were given to creditors in lieu of money.

In 1880 the line was offered to the GWR, which had taken over working from the B&E, and the best price which could be obtained for a line which had cost £50,000 to build was £33,000.

Passenger services were withdrawn from 9 September 1963. The largest user of the line was Wilts United Dairies and up to 30,000 gallons of milk were despatched daily in rail tankers. This traffic continued after the cessation of passenger traffic when the branch was treated as a siding. Before the passenger train service was withdrawn, the fireman used to open the level-crossing gates, which were then closed by the guard following the passage of the train. With the introduction of single-manned diesel locomotives in freight-only times, the guard was responsible for both opening and closing the gates.

The closure of the dairy at Hemyock on 31 October 1975 caused the closure of the branch on the same day and it thus failed by seven months to celebrate its centenary.

Until 1932 locomotive working at Tiverton Junction was interesting as no run-round loop was provided; after arrival an engine had to propel its train into a gravity siding and retire up the branch while the coaches ran back into the platform.

Coldharbour halt opened on 23 February 1929 at a cost of £111 and had a siding until 28 October 1963 when most goods traffic on the branch ceased. Uffculme station, like Culmstock and Hemyock, was of the same basic design – a single platform with a small, red-brick building. Its goods shed was removed in 1932. Wool and hides were despatched. When rabbits were sent on the 5.40 p.m. from Hemyock, the guard phoned Tiverton Junction warning the staff to organize barrows on the branch platform to take the crates to the Up platform for onward transit to London.

NOTICE.

CULME VALLEY
LIGHT RAILWAY.

ON
WEDNESDAY FORENOON, the 15th of MAY, 1872

A
MEETING

WILL BE HELD HERE TO CONSIDER THE PROJECTED SCHEME FOR
FORMING THE PROPOSED LINE.

Any Person who thinks favourably of it is respectfully invited to attend.

RICHD. BOWERMAN,

Dated May 10th, 1872.   LAMBSCROFT, UFFCULME.

Notice of the first public meeting held at the George Inn, Uffculme, to consider proposals for the Culm Valley Light Railway.

Culmstock station was unstaffed from 2 May 1960 and it, too, lost its goods shed in 1932 when a looped siding was put in.

Whitehall halt opened on 27 February 1933 and was much used by anglers. Its shelter was unusually placed at the foot of the platform ramp. A siding was provided beyond.

In the late 1870s a refreshment room was opened at Hemyock to cope with trippers to the Wellington Monument on the Blackdown Hills 3 miles distant; but the excursionists did not materialize and the room was soon closed. Hemyock had goods, carriage and engine sheds and from 1886 a private siding crossed the road to serve the Culm Valley Dairy Co. Before 1916, when it was taken over by Wilts United Dairy Co., its products sent by rail were butter, cheese and condensed milk, but after that date the principal commodity was pasteurized milk for London. From 1932 the liquid milk was sent in glass-lined tanks, the GWR providing the chassis and United Dairies the tanks. Up to twelve 3,000 gallon milk tanks were despatched daily. Locomotives were not permitted over the level-crossing so empty tanks were drawn over by winch and wire cable, the loaded wagons being returned by gravity.

As the B&E, which worked the Culm Valley Light Railway, was a broad gauge line, it had to build at Bristol, two standard gauge 0–6–0Ts, these becoming GWR Nos 1376/7. In 1878 they were replaced by ex-South Devon Railway 2–4–0Ts No. 1298 and No. 1300 used in rotation, one at Hemyock and the other at Exeter. They had started life at Newton Abbot as broad gauge saddle tanks, but were completed at Swindon, where they were changed to standard gauge side tanks. Ex-Watlington & Princes Risborough Railway 2–4–0T No. 1384 arrived on the Culm Valley by 1906, leaving again in 1910. Ex-Cambrian Railways 2–4–0Ts Nos 1192/6 worked in 1927 and No. 1308 *Lady*

55

Margaret, of the same wheel arrangement and from the Liskeard & Looe Railway, in 1929. The 48XX class 0–4–2Ts worked the line from the early 1930s until dieselization when Class 08 shunters were used and then Class 29 diesel-hydraulics and Class 22 diesel-electrics.

The timber-built engine shed at Hemyock closed on 21 October 1929 and the branch locomotive was then shedded at Tiverton Junction. When this shed closed in October 1964, the Hemyock diesel was supplied by Taunton and stabled in Tiverton Junction yard for eleven months.

Coaches used on the branch were particularly interesting. One early vehicle was an ex-Monmouthshire Railways & Canal Company vehicle built in 1848. Only 13 ft in length it had three narrow compartments sharing one lamp. Tight curves due to the line following land boundaries severely restricted types of passenger coaches using the branch. Early this century four-wheel stock was replaced by three short bogie carriages from the Manchester & Milford Railway. These lasted until the 1930s when they were replaced by GWR clerestory coaches. In 1950 two ex-Barry Railway coaches were converted from electric to gas lighting for use on the Culm Valley line as slow speeds on the branch were insufficient for the axle-driven generators to keep the batteries charged. The branch had the last gaslit vehicles on BR. In 1962 these were replaced by ex-LNER coaches whose batteries were replenished overnight by a battery charger at Tiverton Junction. Both vehicles were used on the final passenger trains, and to accommodate extra passengers benches from Tiverton Junction waiting-room were placed in the guard's compartment.

The branch's non-standard loading gauge caused problems. In 1927 a horse-box arrived and cleared the branch loading gauge, but at Hemyock an oil lamp was put in to light the groom's compartment. Protruding above the roof it fouled an overbridge, the lamp was smashed and burning oil set alight bedding and fodder. Fortunately Tiverton Junction was near and the fire was doused and the horse rescued.

The train service varied little over the years. In 1887 the four trains each way took

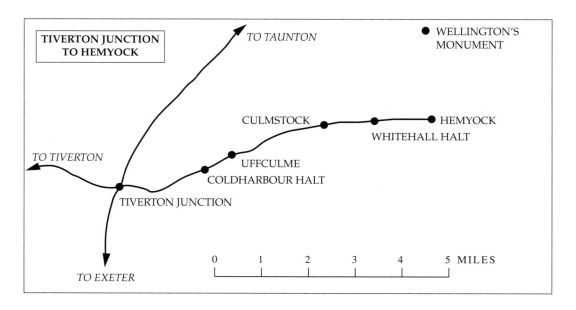

45 minutes which by 1910 had been reduced to 35, a timing which lasted to the end of the branch. Speed was restricted to 15 m.p.h.

When the B&E Act was passed in 1836 a branch line to Tiverton was authorized, but due to a shortage of capital, powers lapsed before it could be built. Another Act was obtained on 31 July 1845. Work started, but was then delayed as an agreement could not be reached with the Grand Western Canal Company. The branch had to pass under the canal at Halberton and the canal, of necessity, had to be closed temporarily while an aqueduct was built to carry the water 40 ft above the railway. The B&E was required to pay £1,200 to the canal company as compensation.

The canal was carried over the line in a cast-iron duct supported on two cast-iron arches, the whole being enclosed with brickwork and the spaces puddled with clay to help prevent leakage. Nevertheless, the crew of the first train of the day in frosty weather had to keep well inside the cab when passing under the aqueduct to avoid being struck by an icicle. Two arches were made so that the line could have been doubled had traffic warranted and for the same reason the fences on the branch were set well back.

Matters were further delayed by a belated deviation at the terminus, but eventually the 4¾ mile long branch was opened on 12 June 1848. Tiverton Road station on the main B&E line was renamed Tiverton Junction.

To prevent undue competition between the railway and the canal resulting in loss to both companies, it was mutually agreed that only the canal should carry lime, and coal traffic should go by rail to Taunton and then by canal. In 1852 this agreement was abandoned and rates for carrying coal were successively reduced until at one time the canal was transporting it free, much to the pleasure of Tiverton inhabitants. The B&E lost an estimated £6,000 on this exercise but, unlike the canal company, could recoup it elsewhere.

The branch was converted to standard gauge on 29 June 1884 in order that a

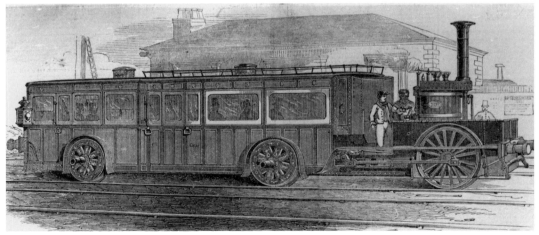

Fairfield steam carriage, named after the builder's works, Fairfield, and built in 1848 by W.B. Adams. As the floor was within 9 in of the rails, passengers could mount from ground level. Notice the luggage rack on the roof.

1848 Courtesy: *Illustrated London News*

connection could be made with the Tiverton & North Devon Railway, which was to be opened on 1 August that year.

With the opening of the Exe Valley line on 1 May 1885, a new station was opened at Tiverton, the old B&E terminus becoming a goods depot. The Tiverton Junction to Tiverton line now provided a shuttle service between the main line and the Exe Valley trains.

About 1890 an old lady dropped sixpence on the line at Tiverton station and insisted on a porter retrieving it before the train started. 'But that official,' reported the *Railway Herald* 'imbued with that strict sense of duty and of punctuality which distinguishes all Great Western officials, said he would give her sixpence of his own and find the lost coin after the train had gone. He suited the action to the word, and the train conveying the lady – who was a stranger – steamed out of the station. Imagine that dutiful and obliging porter's disgust when he found that the dropped coin in the four-foot-way was a bad threepenny-bit!'

The passenger service on the branch was withdrawn on 5 October 1964 and freight from 5 June 1967, the track being lifted in May the following year.

On 5 December 1927 the GWR opened an intermediate halt at Halberton to help combat competition from the bus service. It was situated immediately below a road bridge. Some passengers arrived by cycle and left them on the platform below the bridge to avoid getting a wet saddle.

Running for over a mile on each side of the halt and occupying the site of the second line was a single row of Bramley apple trees. This curious orchard, one tree wide and 2 miles in length, was let by the GWR to Joseph Diggle.

To enable the engine to run round its train at Tiverton Junction, it pushed the coaches up a gravitation siding, uncoupled and ran back clear of the points and then the coaches were run down. The train shed covering the branch coaches was removed when the station was altered in March 1932.

To economize in manpower, trains on the branch consisting of not more than three coaches were permitted to be worked without a guard. To prevent theft, it was required that all luggage, mail and parcels be locked in the luggage compartment. The Tiverton Junction station-master arranged for a porter to work on each trip without a guard, his duties being confined to informing passengers of the arrival of the train at Halberton halt, collecting and issuing any tickets and seeing that all doors were properly closed before the train's departure.

The first train over the branch was hauled by B&E 2–2–2WT No. 58, and a few months later the line could boast that it was probably the first in the country to use a steam railcar. Named *Fairfield*, it was built at Bow by W.B. Adams in 1848. It accommodated sixteen first-class and thirty-two second-class passengers. On test runs with two loaded wagons weighing a total of 31½ tons exclusive of the coach, it managed 27 m.p.h. Eighteen trips were made in 9¼ hours, made up of a running time of 3¾ hours and a standing time of 5½ hours. At first the consumption of coke was 14.8 lb, but this was subsequently reduced to 8.7 lb.

In 1851 *Fairfield* was replaced by small B&E 2–2–2WTs of the No. 30–34 series. Following the gauge conversion 517 class 0–4–2Ts worked passenger trains and 0–6–0STs appeared on goods. These were later withdrawn, replaced by the 48XX (14XX). No. 1442 is preserved in Tiverton Museum as the 'Tivvy Bumper'.

The brick engine shed at Tiverton Junction was renewed in 1932. The 34 ft 6 in turntable was removed in May 1908. Water for locomotive purposes and for cleaning the cattle pens was pumped from Spratford stream by steam pump until 1928, then by a

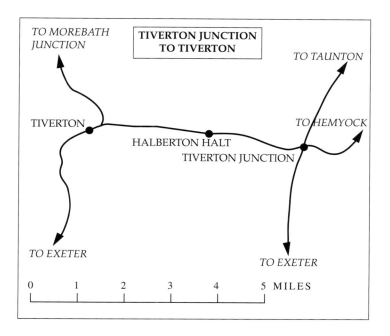

petrol/paraffin set which used petrol initially, switching to paraffin once the engine was warm. An electric pump was installed in 1945. When Exeter closed to steam on 14 October 1963 Tiverton Junction became a sub-shed to Taunton and remained open until 5 October 1964 for the Tiverton branch locomotive. The large water tank at Tiverton was gravity fed from the canal 80 ft above.

In 1850 ten passenger trains ran each way and two on Sundays, in a time of 12 minutes. In 1877 thirteen Down and eleven Up trains were run. In subsequent years the service tended to offer about a dozen trains each way taking 10 minutes, the opening of Halberton adding 2 minutes to the overall journey time.

CULM VALLEY BRANCH.

Narrow Gauge.

Single Line worked by Train Staff.   The Train Staff Stations are Tiverton Junction and Hemyock.

Section.	Form of Staff and Ticket.	Colour of Ticket.
Tiverton Junction and Hemyock.	Square.	Green.

TIVERTON JUNCTION TO HEMYOCK.
Down Trains.

		Week Days only.								
Miles.	STATIONS.	1	2	3	4	5	6	7	8	9
		Pass.	Pass.	Pass.	Pass.					
		A.M.	P.M.	P.M.	P.M.					
	Tiverton Junction .... dep.	9 25	12 30	4 25	7 35	....	....	....	....	..
2	Cold Harbour Siding .. .. ,,	C R	—	—	—	..	..	..	..	..
2¼	Uffculme .... ,,	9 49	12 50	4 44	7 54	....	....	....	....	..
5	Culmstock .... .. ,,	10 4	1 0	4 59	8 9	..	..	..	..	..
6¼	Whitehall Siding .... ,,	C R	—	—	—	..	..	..	..	..
7¼	Hemyock .... arr.	10 20	1 15	5 10	8 20	....	....	....	....	..

HEMYOCK TO TIVERTON JUNCTION.
Up Trains.

		Week Days only.								
Miles.	STATIONS.	1	2	3	4	5	6	7	8	9
		Pass.	Pass.	Pass.	Pass.					
		A.M.	A.M.	P.M.	P.M.					
	Hemyock .... dep.	8 30	10 30	2 35	5 20	....	....	....	....	....
1	Whitehall Siding .... ,,	—	—	—	—					
2¼	Culmstock .. .. .. ,,	8 46	10 46	2 51	5 36	..	..	..	....	..
4¼	Uffculme .... ,,	9 1	11 1	3 6	5 51	....	....	....	....	..
5¼	Cold Harbour Siding .. .. ,,	—	C R			..	..	..	..	..
7¼	Tiverton Junction .... arr.	9 15	11 15	3 20	6 5	..	..	..	..	..

Extract from the Regulations made by the Board of Trade for the working of the
Culm Valley Light Railway.

"That the said Railway shall be worked between Tiverton Junction and Hemyock Station by one Engine in steam combined with the absolute Block Telegraph system; that the rate of speed of the Trains shall not exceed fifteen miles an hour on any part of the said Railway; and that the Locomotive Engines, Carriages and Vehicles used on the Railway shall not have a greater weight than eight tons upon the rails on any one pair of wheels."

B&E timetable, October 1886.

TIVERTON BRANCH.

Narrow Gauge.

Single Line worked by Train Staff. The Train Staff Stations are Tiverton Junction and Tiverton.

Section.	*Form of Staff and Ticket.*	*Colour of Ticket.*
Tiverton Junction and Tiverton.	Round.	Blue.

TIVERTON JUNCTION TO TIVERTON.

Miles.	STATIONS.	Down Trains.					Week Days.					
		1	2	3	4	5	6	7	8	9	10	11
		Goods A	Pass.	Pass.	Pass.	B Pass.	Pass.		Pass.	Pass.	Pass.	Pass.
4¾	Tiverton Junction dep.	A.M. 6 30	A.M. 8 27	A.M. 9 29	A.M. 10 13	A.M. 11 35	P.M. 12 15		P.M. 3 35	P.M. 4 20	P.M. 6 18	A.M. 7 30
	Tiverton .. .. arr.	6 45	8 37	9 39	10 23	11 45	12 25		3 45	4 30	6 28	7 40

Miles.	STATIONS.	Week Days—*continued.*					Sundays.					
		12	13	14	15	16	1	2	3	4	5	6
		Pass.					Engine	Pass.	Pass.	Engine	Pass.	Pass.
4¾	Tiverton Junction dep.	P.M. 10 5					A.M. 8 12	A.M. 8 59	A.M. 10 36	P.M. 3 3	P.M. 4 10	P.M. 5 57
	Tiverton .. .. arr.	10 15					8 22	9 9	10 46	3 13	4 20	6 7

A On Tuesdays this Train will start at 7.10 a.m.   **B** These Trains run on Tuesdays only.

TIVERTON TO TIVERTON JUNCTION.

Miles.	STATIONS.	Up Trains.					Week Days.					
		1	2	3	4	5	7	8	9	11	12	14
		Goods and Pass.	Pass.	Pass.	B Empty Train.	Pass.		Pass.	Pass.	Pass.	Pass.	Pass.
4¾	Tiverton.... .... dep.	A.M. 7 50	A.M. 9 5	A.M. 9 46	A.M. 11 10	A.M. 11 52		P.M. 3 16	P.M. 3 55	P.M. 5 55	P.M. 7 8	P.M. 8 45
	Tiverton Junction arr.	8 2	9 15	9 56	11 20	12 2		3 26	4 5	6 5	7 18	8 55

Miles.	STATIONS.	Week Days—*continued.*					Sundays.					
		16	10	6	13	15	1	2	3	4	5	6
		Engine					Pass.	Pass.	Engine	Pass.	Pass.	Engine.
4¾	Tiverton.... .... dep.	P.M. 10 25					A.M. 8 39	A.M. 10 14	A.M. 11 0	P.M. 3 48	P.M. 5 33	P.M. 6 30
	Tiverton Junction arr.	10 35					8 49	10 24	11 10	3 58	5 43	6 40

B&E timetable, October 1886.

14XX class 0–4–2T No. 1440 leaving Tiverton Junction with the 1.40 p.m. to Hemyock.

12.10.57 R.E. Toop

A train from Hemyock hauled by a 14XX class 0–4–2T arrives at Tiverton Junction. Notice the irregular position of the headlamp. The descent towards the station allows gravity shunting to be used to allow the engine to run round its train.

c. 1960 M.E.J. Deane

Ex-Cambrian Railways 2–4–0T No. 58 *Gladys* as GWR No. 1196, at Uffculme with a train to Hemyock. The newly painted coach is an ex-Manchester & Milford Railway vehicle. The goods shed, left, was removed in 1932. The structure to the right of the chimney is a water tank.

c. 1927 Lens of Sutton

14XX class 0–4–2T No. 1421 at Uffculme with the 2.45 p.m. from Hemyock.

8.6.63 Author

14XX class 0–4–2T No. 1435 and ex-Barry Railway brake third W263W at Culmstock working the 1.40 p.m. from Tiverton Junction.

4.7.56 Hugh Ballantyne

Whitehall halt, with its shelter sited at the foot of the ramp rather than on the platform. One passenger has evidently arrived by cycle. The level-crossing gate in the foreground was opened by the fireman.

c. 1960 Lens of Sutton

14XX class 0–4–2T No. 1421 at Whitehall halt with the 2.45 p.m. from Hemyock. The coach is ex-LNER. Notice the sharply curved siding and the sleeper-built platform wall.

8.6.63 Author

An early view of Hemyock with the former refreshment room behind, and slightly to the right. The three-compartment coaches can be seen on the left. The gate in the foreground gave access to the bank of the River Culm.

c. 1900 Lens of Sutton

2–4–0T No. 1300 at Hemyock with a train of four-wheeled coaches. Construction of No. 1300 began as a broad gauge locomotive at the SDR's works at Newton Abbot, but was completed in 1878 at Swindon as a standard gauge engine. It was withdrawn in May 1934.

c. 1903 Lens of Sutton

14XX 0–4–2T No. 1405 at Hemyock with a mixed train. On the left is the cattle pen.

c. 1960 M.E.J. Deane

14XX class 0–4–2T No. 1466 arriving at Hemyock with the 8.45 a.m. from Tiverton Junction. At least five milk tanks stand in the siding. The signal-box, reduced to a ground frame in 1935, is immediately left of the station building. No. 1466 has been preserved.

19.2.62 Unknown photographer

14XX class 0–4–2T No. 1421 arrives at Hemyock with the 1.42 p.m. from Tiverton Junction.

8.6.63 Author

14XX class 0–4–2T No. 1450 arriving at Tiverton Junction with the 1.20 p.m. from Tiverton.

8.6.63 Author

Halberton halt, view towards Tiverton Junction. The 109 ft long sleeper-walled platform opened on 5 December 1927. It is partly sheltered by the overbridge built wide enough for double track. Notice the ferns growing from the platform wall.

c. 1960 Lens of Sutton

Three 14XX class 0–4–2Ts stand at Tiverton all facing the same direction. Left to right: No. 1471 with the 8.41 a.m. to Tiverton Junction; pushing its train is No. 1442 with the 8.10 a.m. Dulverton to Exeter, St David's; No. 1421 heading the 7.55 Exeter, St David's to Dulverton is taking water.

28.9.63 Hugh Ballantyne

The exterior of Tiverton station.

c. 1905 Author's collection

Stoke Canon to Morebath Junction

Although the Tiverton Junction to Tiverton branch was fine for travellers to Bristol or London, the rail route from Tiverton to Exeter was decidedly circuitous and a direct line was seen to be advantageous. To this end, the Exe Valley Railway received its Act on 30 June 1874, its powers taken over by the B&E the following year. However, no practical steps had been taken by 1876 when the B&E itself was absorbed by the GWR.

In due course, W. Moss of Stafford won the contract for construction of the line, while W.B. Berry of Crediton built the stations at Brampford Speke, Thorverton and Cadeleigh. There were only two cuttings of any significance and about fourteen bridges, most of them of Westleigh stone with Bath stone dressings, though some were built of brick. Additionally there were seventeen viaducts and twenty-four brick or masonry culverts.

The railway opened on 1 May 1885, locomotives being decorated with flowers and flags. As it was Tiverton's third railway the town was quite blasé about it, but festivities were held in Thorverton where a dinner for parishioners was served under an awning erected in the street. The 475 present enjoyed the roast beef, plum puddings and beer. Sports followed and a tea was provided for children and elderly people.

In 1873 the Taunton to Barnstaple line had been opened. When the Exe Valley line was proposed the following year, it was therefore an obvious step to extend the Exe Valley line northwards from Tiverton to link with the Taunton to Barnstaple line at Morebath. The Tiverton & North Devon Railway received its Act on 19 July 1875 and was built by Nathaniel B. Fogg, a Liverpool contractor, with Francis Fox of the B&E acting as chief engineer The first sod was cut on 3 May 1880 by Sir John Heathcoat-Amory, MP for Tiverton and owner of the town's textile mill.

At last all was ready and the line opened on 1 August 1884 some ten months before the Exe Valley Railway. Although worked by the GWR, the Tiverton & North Devon retained its independence as a separate company until 1 July 1894.

Despite a competitive bus service, as recently as the 1950s the Dulverton to Exeter passenger trains were quite well patronized but freight traffic was light. Eventually the line became uneconomic to operate and passenger and goods services were withdrawn on 7 October 1963.

The original station at Stoke Canon was east of the junction with the Exe Valley line and so could not be used by branch trains. To avoid this problem, a new station immediately west of the junction was opened on 2 July 1894, while this in turn was replaced in 1931 by a new five-road station on the same site. It was commonplace, especially at summer weekends, for trains from Dulverton to Exeter to be held at the branch platform at Stoke Canon while a path was found for them either to cross over the Up line, or follow a Down train to Exeter. Stoke Canon closed to passengers on 13 June 1960 and to goods on 3 May 1965.

Brampford Speke halt, originally a station, opened on 1 August 1884. Like all the stations on the line it was built of local stone to a chalet design and had twin gables with decorative barge boards. Temporarily closed on 1 January 1917, it reopened on 1 January 1919 and was unstaffed from 1 October 1923 when it became a halt. Although it now no longer dealt with goods traffic, parcels were still handled in a corrugated iron hut.

Thorverton had a passing loop and a private siding to a mill, grain wagons from Avonmouth being shunted along it by a tractor fitted with a buffer beam. The station closed to goods on 4 May 1964. Sixty-five passengers used the station daily in 1925; this number rose to 170 in 1953 but fell to 92 in 1960. The line from Thorverton to Stoke Canon closed on 30 November 1966 when milk traffic ceased.

Up Exe & Silverton, shortened to Up Exe on 1 May 1905, became a halt when the station was unstaffed on 1 October 1923. The offices were converted to a house and so a corrugated iron waiting shelter was erected at the north end of the platform. From September 1954 only peak period trains called.

Burn halt for Butterleigh, opened on 26 January 1929, was a single platform of stone and concrete blocks, although a wooden shelter with a corrugated iron roof was provided for the comfort of the passengers.

Cadeleigh & Bickleigh, shortened to Cadeleigh on 1 May 1906, had a passing loop. The station closed to goods on 7 October 1963. About 1957 only twenty passengers used it daily, 80 per cent of the station's takings being for freight. Livestock traffic was important, more being despatched than arriving. Sugar beet and timber were also sent away.

West Exe halt opened on 9 March 1928 to serve a suburb of Tiverton and Heathcoat's mill, the town's largest employer. The 109 ft long platform with timber walls surmounted by a timber waiting shed was doubled in length, in concrete, in 1937. At busy times in high summer a porter was sent from Tiverton to sell and collect tickets.

Until the opening of the Exe Valley Railway, trains from Morebath Junction used the original terminal station of the line from Tiverton Junction. When this closed on 1 May 1885 and became part of the goods yard, a new station opened, built a little to the south. This had two through platforms and a terminal bay. In 1912 the layout was modified when the North and South signal-boxes were replaced by a single central box.

On 10 May 1931 the station layout was further improved by having a bay platform added on the eastern side, thus obviating the need for Tiverton Junction trains to cross those of the Exe Valley. On 27 July 1954 the coal yard layout was modified, the short sidings whose only access was by wagon turntable were replaced by sidings at a different angle and reached by points over which locomotives could shunt, thus expediting operations. The gasworks siding was lifted on 29 July 1957.

Tiverton was an important station employing thirty-eight staff in 1950. In 1959 52,592 tickets were issued in addition to 1,055 seasons; 13,174 parcels were despatched and about 88,000 tons of freight handled annually. At the start and end of term, Blundell's School traffic consisted of 400–500 trunks and 200–300 bicycles. The station closed to goods on 5 June 1967.

Bolham halt, opened on 23 April 1928, had a concrete platform 109 ft in length and a corrugated iron shelter with a flat roof. Cove halt, with the only corrugated iron pagoda shelter on the branch, officially opened on 9 June 1924, though there had been a low-platformed Cove Siding halt from March 1923. The siding adjacent to the halt held five wagons and an additional two on the spur. Although the signal-box was reduced to a ground frame in 1923, the 'Cove Siding Signal Box' plate remained until the line's closure. The branch crossed the River Exe on a two-span girder bridge and climbed at

EXE VALLEY BRANCH.

Narrow Gauge.

Single Line worked by Train Staff. The Train Staff Stations are:—Stoke Canon Junction, Thorverton, Cadeleigh, Tiverton, Bampton (Devon), Morebath Junction and Dulverton.

PARTICULARS OF TRAIN STAFFS AND TICKETS:—

SECTION.	Form of Staff and Ticket.	Colour of Ticket.
Stoke Canon Junction and Thorverton ..	Triangular.	White.
Thorverton and Cadeleigh	Round.	Yellow.
Cadeleigh and Tiverton	Oblong.	Blue.
Tiverton and Bampton (Devon)	Square.	Red.
Bampton (Devon) and Morebath Junc.	Triangular.	Green.
Morebath Junction and Dulverton	Round.	White.

Up Trains. EXETER TO DULVERTON.

Miles from Exeter.	STATIONS.		1 A Pass.	2 Pass.	3 Pass.	4 Pass.	5 EV & D & S Goods	6 Pass.	7 Pass.	8	9
			WEEK DAYS ONLY.								
			A.M.	A.M.	A.M.	P.M.	P.M.	P.M.	P.M.		
	Exeter	dep.	7 15	9 45	10 55	1 5	1 40	3 5	6 29		
3½	Stoke Canon Junction	dep.	7 23	9 51	11 3	1 13	X1 50	3 13	6 36		
4¼	Brampford Speke	arr.	7 26	9 54	11 6	1 16	—	3 17	6 38		
		dep.	7 27	9 55	11 7	1 17	—	3 18	6 39		
4¾	Fortescue Crossing	arr.	—	—	—	—	—	—	—		
		dep.	—	—	—	—	—	—	—		
6¼	Thorverton	arr.	7 32	10 X 0	11X12	X1 22	2 0	3 24	6 43		
		dep.	7 35	10 1	11 13	1 23	2 20	3 25	6 44		
6¾	Up Exe Crossing	dep.	—	—	—	—	—	—	—		
7	Up Exe and Silverton ..	arr.	7 38	10 4	11 16	1 26	—	3 28	6 46		
		dep.	7 39	10 5	11 17	1 27	—	3 29	6 47		
10¼	Cadeleigh & Bickleigh....	arr.	7 47	10 12	11 24	1 31	2 33	3 36	6 54		
		dep.	7 49	10 14	11 26	1 36	2 45	3 38	6 55		
14¼	**Tiverton**	arr.	7 59	10 23	X11 35	1 45	X2 56	3 48	7 4		
		dep.	8 4		11 37	1 47	3 25	X3 51	7 6		
19¼	Cove Siding	arr.	—		—	—	—	—	—		
		dep.	—	....	—	—	CR	—	—		
21¼	Bampton (Devon)	arr.	8 18	..	11 51	2 1	•3 45	•4 5	7 20		
		dep.	8 20	....	11 53	2 3	4 30	4 7	7 22		
22¼	Lower Lodfin Crossing	dep.	—	..	—	—	—	—	—		
22¾	Morebath Junction	dep.	8 27	....	12 0	2 10	X4 40	4 15	7 29		
24¾	**Dulverton**	arr.	8X33	..	12 X 5	2 15	X4 45	X4 20	7 35		

A A Station Truck will be worked between Exeter and Dulverton by this Train.

CROSSING ARRANGEMENTS BETWEEN STOKE CANON JUNCTION AND DULVERTON.

The 7.15 a.m. Train from Exeter will cross the 7.35 a.m. Train from Barnstaple at Dulverton.

The 9.45 a.m. Train from Exeter will cross the 9.5 a.m. Train from Dulverton at Thorverton.

The 10.55 a.m. Train from Exeter will cross the 10.50 a.m. Train from Tiverton at Thorverton, the 10.30 a.m. Train from Dulverton at Tiverton, and the 11.25 a.m. Train from Barnstaple at Dulverton.

The 1.5 p.m. Train from Exeter will cross the 12.30 p.m. Train from Dulverton at Thorverton.

The 1.40 p.m. Train from Exeter will cross the 12.30 p.m. Train from Dulverton at Stoke Canon Junction, the 2.40 p.m. Train from Dulverton at Tiverton, shunt for the 3.5 p.m. Train from Exeter at Bampton, cross the 3.40 p.m. Train from Barnstaple at Morebath Junction, and the 4.47 p.m. Train from Dulverton at Dulverton.

The 3.5 p.m. Train from Exeter will cross the 2.40 p.m. Train from Dulverton at Tiverton, will pass the 1.40 p.m. Train from Exeter at Bampton, and cross the 3.40 p.m. Train from Barnstaple at Dulverton.

B&E timetable, October 1886.

EXE VALLEY BRANCH.

Narrow Gauge.

Single Line worked by Train Staff. The Train Staff Stations are:—Stoke Canon Junction, Thorverton, Cadeleigh, Tiverton, Bampton (Devon), Morebath Junction, and Dulverton.

For particulars of the Train Staffs and Tickets see opposite page.

Down Trains. ### DULVERTON TO EXETER.

Miles from Dulverton.	STATIONS.		Week Days Only.								
			1	2	3 D. & S. & E. V. Goods.	4	5	6 Pass. B	7	8	9
			Pass.	Pass.		Pass.	Pass.		Pass.		
			A.M.	A.M.	A.M.	P.M.	P.M.	P.M.	P.M.		
	Dulverton	dep.	X9 5	....	....	10 30	12X30	2X40	X 4 47	X8 0	....	...
2	Morebath Junction	dep.	9 11	....		10 36	12 36	2 46	4 53	8 6	..	..
2½	Lower Lodfin Crossing	dep.	—	....	—						....	....
3½	Bampton (Devon) .. .. {	arr.	9 16	..		10 41	12 41	2 51	4 58	8 11	....	....
		dep.	9 18	....		11 0	12 43	2 53	5 0	8 13	..	..
5½	Cove Siding .... {	arr.	—	..							..	..
		dep.	—		CR	—	—	—	—	—	..	..
10½	Tiverton .. .. .. {	arr.	9 32	..	X11 20	12 57	X 3 7	5 14	8 27		..	..
		dep.	9 35	10 50	11 40	12 59	X3 55	5 17	8 30		..	..
14½	Cadeleigh & Bickleigh .... {	arr.	9 45	11 0	11 52	1 9	4 5	5 27	8 40		..	..
		dep.	9 46	11 1	12 5	1 10	4 6	5 28	8 41		....	....
17¾	Up Exe & Silverton .. .. {	arr.	9 54	11 9	—	1 18	4 14	5 36	8 49		..	..
		dep.	9 55	11 10	—	1 19	4 15	5 37	8 50		..	..
18	Up Exe Crossing	dep.	—		—						..	..
18½	Thorverton .. .. .. {	arr.	9 58	11 13	12 19	1 22	4 18	5 40	8 53		..	..
		dep.	10 X 0	11X14	12 35	1X24	4 19	5 43	8 54		..	..
20	Fortescue Crossing .... {	arr.	—		—						..	..
		dep.	—		—	—	—	—			..	..
20½	Brampford Speke .. .. {	arr.	10 5	11 19	—	1 29	4 24	5 48	9 0		..	..
		dep.	10 7	11 21	—	1 31	4 26	5 50	9 2		..	..
21¼	Stoke Canon Junction	dep.	10 11	11 25	12 46	X 1 35	4 29	5 53	9 5		..	..
24¾	Exeter	arr.	10 18	11 33	12 55	1 42	4 36	6 0	9 12		..	..

B A Station Truck will be worked between Dulverton and Exeter by this Train.

CROSSING ARRANGEMENTS BETWEEN DULVERTON AND STOKE CANON JUNCTION.

The 9.5 a.m. train from Dulverton will cross the 7.55 a.m. train from Taunton at Dulverton, and the 9.45 a.m. Train from Exeter at Thorverton.

The 10.50 a.m. Train from Tiverton will cross the 10.55 a.m. Train from Exeter at Thorverton.

The 10.30 a.m. Train from Dulverton will cross the 10.55 a.m. Train from Exeter at Tiverton.

The 12.30 p.m. train from Dulverton will cross the 11.20 a.m. train from Taunton at Dulverton, the 1.5 p.m. Train from Exeter at Thorverton, and the 1.40 p.m. train from Exeter at Stoke Canon Junction.

The 2.40 p.m. train from Dulverton will cross the 1.30 p.m. train from Taunton at Dulverton, and the 1.40 and 3 5 p.m. Trains from Exeter at Tiverton.

The 4.47 p.m. Train from Dulverton will cross the 1.40 p.m. Train from Exeter at Dulverton.

The 8.0 p.m. Train from Dulverton will cross the 6.55 p.m. Train from Taunton at Dulverton.

B&E timetable, October 1886.

1 in 63 to Bampton, which had two platforms, a passing loop and fair-sized goods yard with two sidings serving a quarry. Until June 1911 its nameboards proclaimed Bampton, but that month they were changed to Bampton (Devon) to avoid confusion with Bampton, Oxfordshire, on the Oxford to Witney line. Sixty to seventy passengers used the station daily in the 1930s and this figure rose to 200 in the early fifties. When Bampton Pony Fair was held the animals were despatched in forty to fifty cattle wagons, but this traffic was lost to road about 1947.

Beyond the station the line climbed at 1 in 66 to Morebath Junction, passing Lower Lodfin Crossing signal-box on the way. This signal-box was manned by Signalwoman Town for twenty-three years, spanning the end of the last century to the beginning of this one – a period when it was most unusual for a woman to carry out such a job. Although fifty wagon trains were permitted Bampton to Exeter, there was a limit of twenty-eight Dulverton to Bampton, but trains rarely, if ever, reached this length.

Morebath Junction halt, opened on 1 December 1928, originally had a sleeper wall, later replaced with concrete blocks, behind which material was tipped to platform level. The platform shelter was unusual in having a canopy. It was reached through fields and when it was wet underfoot, passengers would wear boots, carry their shoes and change in the shelter, leaving their boots under the bench ready for their return.

Only tank engines were normally utilized on the 19¼ mile long branch because of the short turntable at Dulverton, but a tender engine, chimney first, was allowed to work a through train. When the main line Exeter to Taunton was blocked, and the Hele & Bradninch area flooded fairly frequently, main line trains were diverted over the Exe Valley line, usually Up trains proceeding Tiverton to Tiverton Junction and Down trains via Dulverton. Although the Exe Valley had a Yellow classification, in an emergency the larger Prairie tank engines could be used unassisted, or a Mogul, which could be assisted providing the latter led. During the Second World War some non-military freight was sent from Exeter to Taunton via Dulverton to free the main line for essential traffic. During the same period Exe Valley signal-boxes remained open all night so they could be ready in case of emergency diversions. In 1944 a bomb at Hele caused all traffic to be diverted, the Up and Down Cornish Riviera expresses crossing at Bampton.

In the early days, 517 class 0–4–2Ts hauled trains of three four-wheeled coaches, while from 1923 auto-working was used. In 1932 48XX class 0–4–2Ts appeared and latterly 0–6–0PTs of the 36XX, 57XX and 64XX classes and 45XX 2–6–2Ts. Auto-coaches, including that named *Thrush*, were usually hauled from Exeter. On the last day of passenger working, and a week before Exeter shed closed to steam, diesel-hydraulic Class 22 hauled six coaches.

The locomotive shed at Stoke Canon was almost end-on to the goods shed. It closed in 1879 and was converted into a goods shed in 1894.

Initially the train service showed little variation. In 1885 five trains ran each way between Exeter and Dulverton taking 1 hour 10 minutes and an additional train worked from Exeter to Tiverton and back. The four trains in 1920 took 1 hour 5 minutes. The branch was subject to a speed limit of 35 m.p.h. The introduction of auto-working gave a much more intensive service, but the opening of new halts added to the journey time. In 1930 eight trains ran each way taking 1 hour 15 minutes. Three trains ran each way on Sundays between Exeter and Tiverton, with through working from the branch to Newton Abbot on certain Sundays.

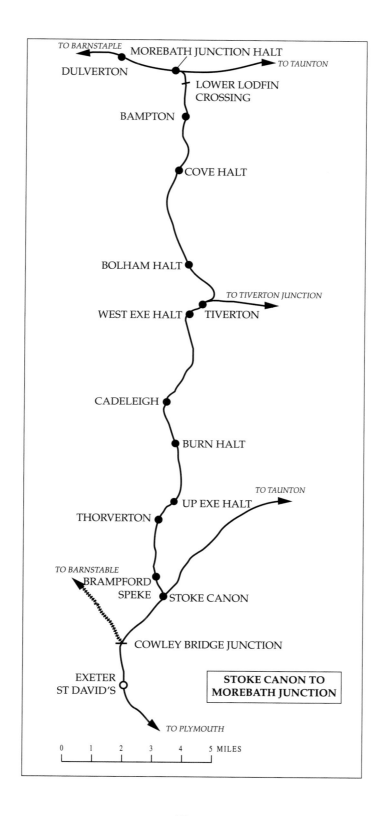

TO BARNSTAPLE

MOREBATH JUNCTION HALT

TO TAUNTON

DULVERTON

LOWER LODFIN
CROSSING

BAMPTON

COVE HALT

BOLHAM HALT

TO TIVERTON JUNCTION

WEST EXE HALT   TIVERTON

CADELEIGH

BURN HALT

TO TAUNTON

UP EXE HALT

THORVERTON

TO BARNSTABLE

BRAMPFORD
SPEKE

STOKE CANON

COWLEY BRIDGE JUNCTION

EXETER
ST DAVID'S

STOKE CANON TO
MOREBATH JUNCTION

TO PLYMOUTH

0   1   2   3   4   5 MILES

14XX class 0–4–2T No. 1421 arrives at Cadeleigh with the 1.45 p.m. Saturdays-only Tiverton to Exeter, St David's.

28.9.63 Hugh Ballantyne

55XX class 2–6–2T No. 5524 at Tiverton. On the left is 14XX class 0–4–2T No. 1452.

c. 1959 Photographer unknown

Starkey, Knight & Ford Brewery's Foden steam lorry in the goods yard at Tiverton.

1928 Author's collection

Cove, view towards Tiverton. The signal-box to the left of the level-crossing was reduced to a ground frame in July 1923. Beyond is the quarry.

c. 1955 M.E.J. Deane

77

1854 class 0–6–0ST No. 1873 at Bampton.

c. 1905 Author's collection

North British diesel-hydraulic D6318 about to leave with the 3.20 p.m. Bampton to Exeter, St David's.

28.9.63 Hugh Ballantyne

14XX class 0–4–2T No. 1466 passes Lower Lodfin Crossing with the 10.25 a.m. Exeter, St David's to Dulverton.

8.6.63 Author

A Down train being waved away from Morebath Junction halt.

c. 1960 T.J. Saunders

Heathfield to Exeter

The Teign Valley Railway Act received Royal Assent on 13 July 1863 to build a line from Heathfield to Chudleigh and Doddiscombsleigh. Subsequent Acts were passed to raise further capital, make deviations and postpone work. Messrs Walker were appointed contractors but the GWR did not open the standard gauge line to Ashton, with a siding beyond to Teign House, until 9 October 1882. As the Moretonhampstead branch was still broad gauge at this date, there was no physical junction at Heathfield, the new branch being isolated from the GWR system.

The Exeter, Teign Valley & Chagford Railway Act of 20 August 1883 authorized a line from Exeter to Christow to link with the branch from Heathfield. Capital was slow coming in and the building contract with James & John Dickson was not signed until the end of 1893, the first sod being cut by Lady Northcote on 7 November 1894. There were still financial problems and powers had to be revived by the Company's Act of 12 August 1898 which authorized a change of name to the Exeter Railway Company. The line opened on 1 July 1903, a celebratory luncheon being held in a marquee at the Alphington Road goods depot, Exeter. The first train carried three hundred passengers in eleven coaches drawn by 1854 class 0–6–0ST No. 1873 decked with flags and foliage.

The complete route from Exeter to Heathfield was worked by the GWR and known as the Teign Valley branch. Both the Exeter and the Teign Valley railways were absorbed by the GWR from 1 July 1923. During the Second World War ambulance trains worked over the branch hauled by LNER inside cylinder B12 class 4–6–0s.

The 15¾ mile long branch curved west from the main line at Exeter Railway Junction just west of St Thomas Viaduct, and at Alphington Road Goods Junction a line trailed in from the five-road goods depot, while two lines served the Exeter Corporation Cattle Market. The latter had two loading platforms built in October 1939 allowing twenty-eight cattle trucks to be loaded simultaneously, as well as meat from the abbatoir. Each Friday 500 to 600 cattle were loaded, and up to 100 on Mondays.

At Exeter Basin Loop Junction a spur opened on 2 May 1904 which passed under the main line and joined the Exeter Basin line. In March 1958, about ½ mile from Exeter Railway Junction, a trailing branch was thrown off the stub of the Teign Valley line and trailed to the Marsh Barton Trading Estate to serve Messrs Cadbury/Fry and E. Pearce & Co. Traffic for Fry's ended in 1971, but at the time of writing, on three Saturdays out of four, a train of about thirty wagons of scrap leaves Marsh Barton sidings. Latterly it has been Class 60 hauled, but Class 56 worked it previously.

Alphington halt opened on 2 April 1928, a 100 ft long wooden platform with a flat-roofed corrugated iron shelter. From here the line ascends for 4 miles at 1 in 56.

Ide station, brick built as were all the others on the branch, was sited on the north side of the line and had the advantage of being at the centre of the village. Closed from

80

1 January 1917 to 1 May 1919, it was down-graded to a halt sometime prior to June 1928. Its siding was lifted in 1955. The line passed through Perridge Tunnel, 836 yd, with Longdown station just beyond its western portal.

Longdown, at the line's summit, had a looped siding and between 19 September 1943 and 1954 a 1,100 ft running loop was in place, vital for passing trains when the main line from Newton Abbot to Exeter was blocked. These additions during the Second World War resulted in the station having four ground frames as well as the existing signal-box. Drinking water was brought by train from Trusham. Beyond the station the line descended for 3 miles at 1 in 64 before plunging into the 248 yd long Culver Tunnel.

Dunsford halt, 2 miles distant from the village, opened on 16 January 1928. It had a single platform on the south side of the line, and a corrugated iron shelter with an unusual sloping roof. Christow had two platforms, a passing loop extended 21 May 1943, quarry sidings and water cranes. In springtime, excursions used to be run to this station as wild daffodils grew in abundance in the locality. The permanent way gang had its headquarters at Christow, a small, petrol-driven inspection car being provided for the ganger, and a motor trolley for carrying the men and a small quantity of tools. Additional tools were taken on a trailer. When Christow was the terminus of the line from Heathfield it was known as Teign House and the line from Ashton operated as a siding.

While constructing the Exeter Railway just north of the station J.H. Dickson discovered basalt and formed the Devon Basalt & Granite Company. A Manning Wardle 0–4–0ST, purchased about 1911, and *Alderman*, a Lilleshaw 0–4–0ST, worked the siding, which closed about 1932.

South of Christow the line bridged the River Teign and shortly beyond, Ryecroft Quarry siding trailed in.

Ashton had a platform on the west side and a low station building. Its sidings were lifted on 1 September 1957. At one time the terminus of the branch from Heathfield, it had a brick-built engine shed with a 50 ft long pit inside, and a 25 ft pit in front of the coal stage. Opened in October 1882, it was probably closed around 1908. On 1 January 1901 0–4–2T No. 540 was shedded there. The building was not demolished until 1960.

Whetcombe Quarry siding, ⅓ mile north of Trusham, was in use from 1909 to 1952. Trusham originally had a single platform on the west side of the line, but the loop siding was extended and converted to passenger use and a Down platform with concrete waiting shelter was added, these improvements being brought into use on 8 July 1943. Beyond the station the line crossed the River Teign and at Crockham sidings ground frame, sidings trailed in from the Teign Valley Granite Company, which owned 0–4–0ST *Finetta*, built by Avonside in 1911 and worked until about 1916. Three travelling cranes were also used for shunting.

Chudleigh had a single platform on the east side of the line, its timber building covered with sand and buff paint. As it was close to the River Teign the station approach was liable to flooding; a raised gangway from an adjacent lane led to a special timber-built platform for use on such occasions.

Chudleigh Knighton halt opened on 9 June 1924 at a cost of £300, its corrugated iron pagoda shelter standing on a masonry platform. To the south were sidings brought into use by the Ministry of Food on 22 August 1943. They were lifted around 1952. Heathfield station is described in the chapter on the Moretonhampstead line.

The first locomotives to work on the branch were 517 class 0–4–2Ts; steam railmotors came in the 1920s and 45XX 2–6–2Ts in the late twenties, the railmotors being withdrawn in 1935. In the thirties 48XX class 0–4–2Ts worked auto-trains. Auto-trailer No. 215, ex-steam railmotor No. 98, was the last used regularly. Auto-workings on the branch ceased in September 1957 and for the rest of the line's existence, Exeter and Newton Abbot passenger sets were used on economical programmes. 57XX class 0–6–0PTs were used on goods trains, and after the line was cut back to Trusham, 41XX and 45XX class 2–6–2Ts worked quarry trains. When the branch was used for the diversion of main line trains, 43XX class 2–6–0s handled them, as necessary banked by class 45XX 2–6–2Ts.

In 1934 camping coaches were introduced at Ashton, followed later by vehicles at Chudleigh and Ide. As an average of only 193 passengers used the branch daily, passenger services were withdrawn on 9 June 1958, even though Ashton station had been repainted that April. Also on 9 June 1958 Marsh Barton to Christow closed completely. Christow and Ashton closed on 1 May 1961 following serious flooding near Ashton which washed away an embankment. Trusham closed on 5 April 1965 and Chudleigh on 4 December 1967.

The opening timetable in 1882 provided four trains each way between Newton Abbot and Chudleigh; in 1910 there were five trains between Exeter and Heathfield, plus three Exeter to Heathfield. In 1957 five ran each way, plus one Exeter to Trusham and another on Saturdays. Also on Saturdays one train ran from Heathfield to Alphington halt and back. A road connection was made between Alphington and St Thomas' and St David's stations, the timetable stating the link was by 'Exeter Corporation Omnibus, heavy luggage not conveyed'. This train terminated at Alphington because of severe congestion on the main line at St David's.

RUNNING OF TRAINS THROUGH FLOODED AREAS—TRUSHAM AND HEATHFIELD.

The following instructions apply in regard to the emergency working to be adopted when the line is flooded between Trusham and Heathfield :

The flood area between the above points usually extends from 80 yards on the Trusham side of Chudleigh Station overbridge to 150 yards on the Heathfield side of Chudleigh Station overbridge.

The Porter at Chudleigh, upon observing the area becoming flooded, must immediately get into touch with the Engineering Department.

If the area is safe for the passage of trains, immediate steps must be taken to advise the person in charge at Heathfield and Trusham, also the Exeter Station Master. Drivers of trains leaving for the flooded area must be advised to proceed cautiously.

If the Engineering Department find it necessary to prohibit trains passing through the flooded area, Down trains must work to and from the Emergency Platform on the Trusham side of Chudleigh Station, and a road motor service be maintained between Chudleigh and Heathfield, the Station Master at Christow to be responsible for obtaining a fully licensed passenger-carrying vehicle, if possible from the Devon General Omnibus Company.

Trains working to and from the Emergency Platform at Chudleigh must be signalled in accordance with Electric Train Token Regulation 8.A., and the Driver advised that the train is to work to and from Chudleigh Emergency Platform only.

Auto trains only must work over the Branch whilst the line is flooded.

Regulation for running of trains through flooded area around Chudleigh. From *GWR Appendix to Service Time Tables, Exeter Division*, 1947.

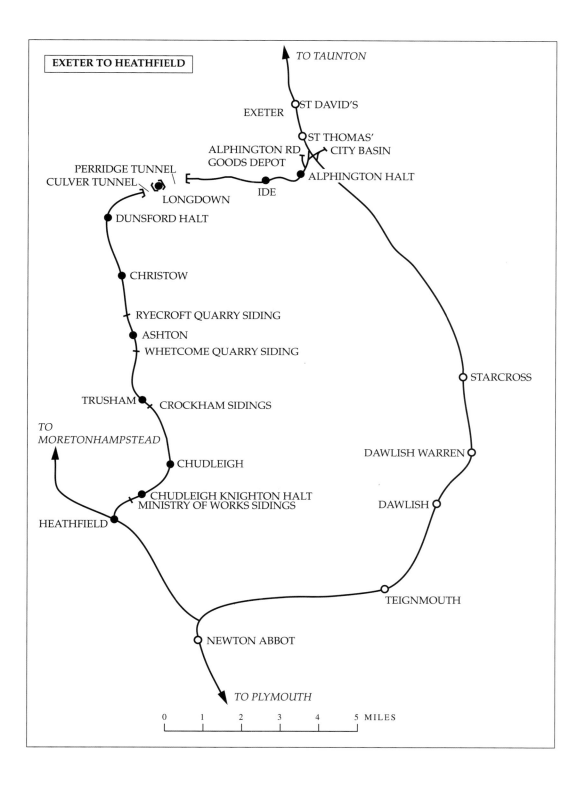

EXETER TO HEATHFIELD

TO TAUNTON

EXETER ◯ ST DAVID'S

◯ ST THOMAS'
ALPHINGTON RD ⊢ CITY BASIN
GOODS DEPOT
PERRIDGE TUNNEL
CULVER TUNNEL
● IDE ● ALPHINGTON HALT
LONGDOWN

● DUNSFORD HALT

● CHRISTOW

┼ RYECROFT QUARRY SIDING
● ASHTON
┼ WHETCOME QUARRY SIDING

STARCROSS ◯

TRUSHAM ● ✕ CROCKHAM SIDINGS

TO
MORETONHAMPSTEAD

DAWLISH WARREN ◯

● CHUDLEIGH

● CHUDLEIGH KNIGHTON HALT
MINISTRY OF WORKS SIDINGS
DAWLISH ◯

HEATHFIELD ●

TEIGNMOUTH ◯

◯ NEWTON ABBOT

TO PLYMOUTH

0   1   2   3   4   5 MILES

83

An Exeter, St David's to Heathfield train climbing to Longdown.

22.3.58 P.Q. Treloar

A busy scene at Christow with 14XX class 0–4–2T No. 1451 working the 12.49 p.m. Heathfield to Exeter, St David's, crossing 57XX 0–6–0PT No. 7761 in black livery heading the 12.45 p.m. Exeter, St David's to Heathfield. Near the shelter on the Down platform can be seen a water crane. It was unusual for one to be sited towards the centre of the platform.

15.2.58 Hugh Ballantyne

517 class 0–4–2T No. 552 at Christow with an Exeter, St David's, to Heathfield train of three coaches, the centre one having a clerestory roof. No. 552 was withdrawn in May 1915.

c. 1910 Author's collection

45XX class 2–6–2T No. 5530 taking on water at Christow while working a Down train.

c. 1960 P.Q. Treloar collection

55XX class 2–6–2T No. 5530 leaving Ashton on an Up train. The wicket gate was kept open for pedestrians longer than the main gate.

c. 1960 P.Q. Treloar collection

The thrice weekly 10.55 a.m. pick-up goods from Newton Abbot at Trusham. The Cementflo wagons are worked by 57XX 0–6–0PT No. 3659.

10.8.61 Hugh Ballantyne

A steam railmotor at Chudleigh. A gradient post is in the left foreground.

c. 1932 Lens of Sutton

A 517 class 0–4–2T enters Chudleigh with a five-coach Heathfield to Exeter, St David's train. The yard crane has timber beams.

c. 1910 Author's collection

Heathfield, view Down. The Candy & Co's pottery siding is on the left and the Teign Valley branch on the right. The signal-box depicted here was replaced in 1916. An unidentified tank engine is shunting. The end of the timber station building has advertisements for: Western Times; W & A. Gilbey's Old Spey; Beechwood hams; Hudson's soap; Sunny Island Ceylon tea and K boots and shoes.

c. 1905 Lens of Sutton

Heathfield, view Down. The 2–6–2T, left, is on the Mortonhampstead branch and the Teign Valley auto-trailer carries a 'Tiverton' destination board.

c. 1932 Lens of Sutton

Heathfield, view Up. The engine is Metro class 2–4–0T No. 3590, withdrawn in April 1944. The trailer adjacent to the locomotive is No. 156, formerly steam rail motor No. 89.

22.7.39 Lens of Sutton

Heathfield, view Down.

10.5.58 Author's collection

Newton Abbot to Moretonhampstead

The 12¼ mile long broad gauge Moretonhampstead & South Devon Railway received its Act of Parliament on 7 July 1862. From south of Bovey to Teigngrace the new railway followed the line of the Haytor Tramway, Devon's first permanent railway. Constructed by George Templar, this opened on 16 September 1820 carrying granite from Haytor to north of Teigngrace where the stone was transhipped to a barge on the Stover Canal and transferred to a sea-going vessel at Teignmouth. The rarity of the line was that its rails were of granite, with a flange on the inside, set at a gauge of 4 ft 3 in. The line descended 1,200 ft in 9 miles. The wagons were abut 13 ft in length and had a 10 ft wheelbase; the wheels were 2 ft in diameter, were loose on the axles and had treads 3 in wide. Parts of the tramway can be followed toady, and it is now designated an Ancient Monument. The Haytor Vale to Manaton road crosses the tramway at OS grid reference SX 769776 and about ½ mile west can be seen some granite points. Haytor granite was used for building London Bridge, the British Museum and the National Gallery, but eventually granite was obtained from cheaper sources and in 1858 the tramway fell into disuse.

Local folk were slow to subscribe to the Moretonhampstead line and bad weather delayed Brassey & Ogilvie, the contractors, but eventually the branch opened on 4 July 1866 and was worked by the SDR, which absorbed it on 1 July 1872. It was converted to standard gauge between 20 and 23 May 1892. A special train left Bristol at 9.55 a.m. on 19 May carrying 462 men. At Newton Abbot the train was divided, part going to Moretonhampstead, arriving at 4.45 p.m., and the rest travelling to Kingswear. A standard gauge train took the men home, leaving Moretonhampstead at 6.40 a.m. on 24 May. The previous day the first public standard gauge passenger train on the branch consisted of four six-wheelers, two first- and second-class composites and two brake thirds. The gauge conversion saved £144 a year on transfer expenses at Heathfield.

BR claimed that the branch lost £17,000 yearly so the passenger service was withdrawn from 2 March 1959. Moretonhampstead closed to goods on 6 April 1964, and Bovey on 6 July 1970. It still remains open to Heathfield dealing with china clay and oil.

The branch leaves the main line east of Newton Abbot station immediately before crossing the River Lemon, and beyond on the west side were the power station sidings in use between August 1928 and April 1968. Beyond Whitelake Bridge are sidings and a ball clay siding. When the new goods depot was opened on 12 June 1911, the track was doubled from the junction to the depot. Teignbridge level-crossing has gates which are normally padlocked, and opened by the shunter. The former crossing-keeper's cottage, condemned in 1947 as unfit for human habitation and latterly used as a cabin, is still extant. From 1892 until 1965 there were clay sidings south of the level-crossing.

Teigngrace station opened in December 1867, a single platform on the west side of the line with a small brick-built office. It closed from 1 January 1917 until 1 May 1919 as a wartime economy measure. It was unstaffed on 8 May 1939.

Heathfield was called Chudleigh Road until 1 October 1882. When the standard gauge line to Ashton opened, the broad gauge Moretonhampstead branch platform became an island. On 9 June 1927 a crossing loop and Down platform were added. A double-track junction was brought into use on 9 May 1943 to aid the branch's use as a diversionary route. Geest Industries Limited had a private siding from February 1961 until December 1975. In June 1965 Gulf Oil sidings, ½ mile north of the station, were brought into use, and beyond the headshunt the line is now lifted.

Bovey Granite siding and Bovey Pottery siding were passed before reaching Brimley halt, opened on 21 May 1928 with a timber waiting shelter and unusually two benches on the platform. Bovey had two platforms and these were lengthened at their northern end about 1894. From 22 July 1927 reversible working could be instituted over the Down platform road.

The branch climbed on a ruling gradient of 1 in 67 to Hawkmoor halt, which opened on 27 May 1931 and was renamed Pullabrook on 13 June 1955. Until the early 1950s patients for Hawkmoor Sanatorium arrived at the halt by rail and then were conveyed to the hospital by horse-drawn vehicle. The gradient steepened to 1 in 58 before Lustleigh, which had a single platform and siding which in the thirties accommodated a camping coach. Unusually, a visitors' book was kept in the station waiting-room. In 1931 the station was temporarily renamed Baskerville while filming took place for Conan Doyle's novel. This featured 2–4–0T Metro tank No. 3590 and 2–6–2T No. 5530. It is believed that this was the first time a 'talkie' film was made featuring a train in motion. The special consisted of the locomotive, a Hydra D well-wagon holding the film crew's generating lorry, buffet brake first No. 8303, built in 1911 for the Plymouth boat trains, and first-class saloon No. 9004, built in June 1930 and which had been recently used by Charlie Chaplin.

Another unusual feature of Lustleigh station was a small gravestone bearing the epitaph:

Beneath this stone and stretched out flat
Lies Jumbo, once our station cat.

The gradient steepened to 1 in 49 to reach Moretonhampstead 550 ft above Newton Abbot. There was a wooden train shed and stone station buildings. In June 1925 the GWR erected a commemorative stone, like a gravestone, alongside the station approach path, displaying the legend: 'Moretonhampstead and South Devon Railway 1866. Directors: Earl of Devon; Thomas Wills; William R. Hole; Joseph Divett; Elias Cuming; Thomas Woollcombe'. The station was gas lit, supplies being obtained from the works at the station throat. There was a stone goods shed. Cattle and sheep were despatched as well as train loads of potatoes. After the Second World War there was lignite traffic. A horse bus to Chagford was subsidized by the GWR for many years at £133 per annum. On 9 April 1906 the GWR started its own service, the Milnes-Daimler bus connecting with trains. From 12 July 1909 tours were run to Princetown and Dartmeet. Vehicles were kept in a garage in the station yard. These services were taken over by the Western National Omnibus Company in 1929.

The GWR also owned the Manor House Hotel, opened in 1930 at Moretonhampstead. It had been built in 1907 for Viscount Hambledon, head of W.H. Smith & Sons. The consultant architect was Detmar Blow and the site architect Walter Mills. Jacobean in style, the hotel was extended in 1935 to give a total of sixty-six bedrooms. In the autumn

MANOR HOUSE HOTEL

MORETONHAMPSTEAD (Devon)
(Under the Management of the Great Western Railway)

18-HOLE GOLF COURSE IN HOTEL GROUNDS

This hotel is ideally situated on the edge of Dartmoor, 700 feet above sea-level, and has its own grounds of 200 acres of park and pleasure lands. Central heating and electric lighting are installed throughout the building, and the drainage and water supply are of modern type. The hotel is fully licensed.

Trout-fishing in the River Bovey on the estate and Trout and Salmon fishing in the River Teign. Tennis on hard and grass courts, croquet, bathing pool. A very fine 18-hole golf course (5,571 yds.) has been constructed in the hotel grounds.

Winter terms : 4½, 5½, 6 and 7 guineas per week, including meals, accommodation, baths, early morning and afternoon teas. Garage accommodation for 20 cars, including 10 lock-up garages. Nearest station Moretonhampstead (2 miles). Hotel 'Bus meets principal trains.

Illustrated Brochure obtainable from Hotel Manager or Mr. G. J. Walker, Great Western Royal Hotel, Paddington Station, London, W.2.

Telegrams : "Manorotel, North Bovey."   'Phone : Moretonhampstead 55.

Advert for GWR hotel. From GWR publication of the 1930s, *Holiday Haunts*.

of 1940 it was requisitioned by the government and used as an army hospital. Ambulance trains headed by LNER B12 class 4–6–0s ran up the branch as the low axle loading of the these locomotives enabled them to work over routes banned to other engines of their size. The hotel, which had an eighteen-hole golf-course in its grounds, was reopened to visitors on 1 October 1946. BR sold it in 1983.

At first the branch was worked by Hawthorn class 2–4–0ST *Penn* and 4–4–0STs. Following the narrowing of the gauge, trains were headed by 0–6–0STs, 517 class 0–4–2Ts and Metro 2–4–0Ts while by 1914 45XX 2–6–2Ts had appeared. Collett 48XX class 0–4–2Ts worked auto-trains from 1939 and towards the end BR Standard Class 3MT 2–6–2Ts. Branch locomotives usually faced Moretonhampstead. The stone-built locomotive shed at Moretonhampstead unusually had a brick signal-box built against its side. The water tank was gravity fed from a nearby farm.

In 1911 the branch train consisted of an A-set, the six-wheel stock comprising a brake third, two compos, a third and a brake third. That same year a through coach was run to and from Paddington. Between April 1940 and December 1945 auto-trains consisted of Clifton Down compartment-type control trailer No. 3331, normally working with intermediate trailer No. 3275. Both were withdrawn the following year.

In 1887 the train service consisted of five trains each way and two on Sundays, taking about 40 minutes. The timetable for 1910 showed the same number of trains but taking 5 minutes less. In 1922 eight trains ran each way, plus one from Newton Abbot to Bovey and back. Half of these trains came from Kingswear, Paignton and Plymouth, though most only returned to Newton Abbot. No trains were run on Sundays. Sunday passenger trains began again on 3 June 1923, as many as eight return trips being made by 1935 and at one time a through train was run to Torbay. In 1938 eleven trains ran each way daily, plus six from Newton Abbot to Bovey. There were eight to Moretonhampstead on Sundays.

In 1925 the daily branch freight traffic averaged twenty-two wagons of coal and minerals forwarded and eleven received; fifteen of general goods forwarded and eight received. Annually 1,699 milk churns were carried and 423 trucks of livestock.

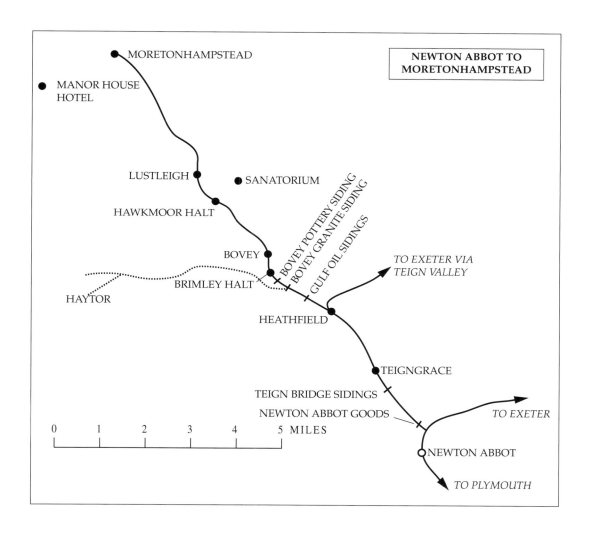

Railfreight Class 50 50149 waits at Teignbridge for a train crewman to return from locking the crossing gates while working the Heathfield to Tavistock Junction goods, comprising two china clay 'Tiger' tanks.

28.7.88 Hugh Ballantyne

A 44XX class 2–6–2T draws a Moretonhampstead to Newton Abbot train into Heathfield. The track is on longitudinal sleepers. Messrs Candy's Brick & Tile Works are prominent. The end of the wooden station building advertises: BDV tobacco; Van Houten's cocoa; Sunny Island Ceylon tea; Beechwood hams and a firm which vacuum-cleaned carpets.

c. 1910 M.E.J. Deane collection

14XX class 0–4–2T No. 1472 enters Heathfield with a Moretonhampstead to Newton Abbot train.
22.3.58 P.Q. Treloar

A collection of GWR charabancs at Bovey. Left is No. 238, registration T 7692, with an AEC 3½ ton chassis, going to Haytor Rocks. No. 857, registration XY 2110 is a Burford 30 cwt and is bound for Becky Falls and Manaton. Two more GWR charabancs are in the background.
c. 1925 Author's collection

A Metro class 2–4–0T enters Lustleigh with a Down train of five coaches. The disused signal-box stands on the platform. Land on the left, here used as a station garden, allowed for a second platform to be built.

c. 1910 Lens of Sutton

5101 class 2–6–2T No. 4174 enters Lustleigh with an Up train. Notice the camping coach on the left and the railwaymen's allotments, right.

1.11.58 Author's collection

Generator set for filming *The Hound of the Baskervilles* stands on a Hydra D well-wagon at Lustleigh.

1931 Author's collection

Lustleigh, temporarily renamed 'Baskerville' during filming.

1931 Author's collection

Inside Moretonhampstead train shed, view Up.

c. 1910 A.J.F. Bond

BR Standard Class 3 2–6–2T No. 82032 at Moretonhampstead with auto-trailer W224W and W234W working the 11.35 a.m. to Newton Abbot.

21.12.55 Hugh Ballantyne

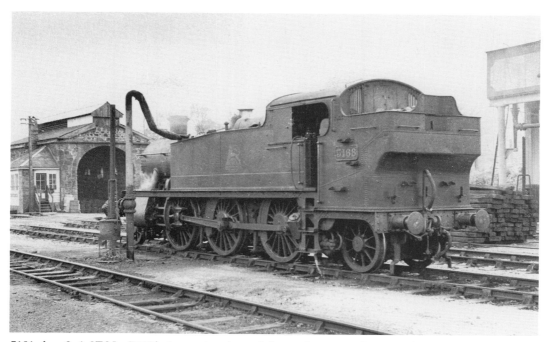

5101 class 2–6–2T No. 5168 being watered near Moretonhampstead engine shed.

22.3.58 P.Q. Treloar

5101 class 2–6–2T No. 5168 at Moretonhampstead awaiting departure to Newton Abbot.

22.3.58 P.Q. Treloar

Points on the Haytor Tramway near Haytor.

18.7.94 Author

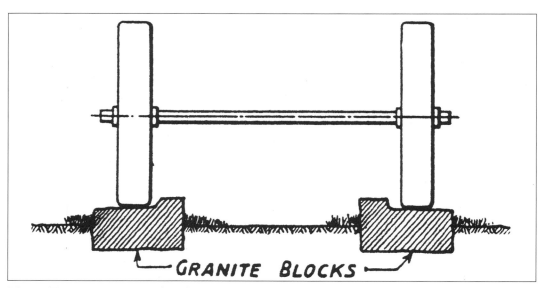

GRANITE BLOCKS

Haytor Tramway – section of track and wheels. (Courtesy *Railway Magazine*)

Newton Abbot to Kingswear

The SDR Act of 28 August 1848 allowed a line to be built from Aller Junction, west of Newton Abbot, to Torre. The single broad gauge line opened to passengers on 18 December 1848, the first train being hauled by *Taurus*, a GWR Leo class 2–4–0. Two hundred passengers were carried in nine first-class and fifteen second-class coaches, the 6 mile trip taking 13 minutes. The line opened to goods on 6 October 1849.

The branch was continued to Kingswear under powers obtained by the Dartmouth & Torbay Railway Act of 27 July 1857. This company was supported by Charles Seale Hayne, who sponsored river steamers to feed the SDR at Totnes and also founded the nearby agricultural college. The first sod of the Kingswear line was cut on 21 January 1858.

The opening to Paignton on 2 August 1859 involved the construction of twenty bridges, a viaduct and a 133 yd long tunnel. The opening was celebrated with a large baked pudding; made in eight portions and then put together it weighed a total of 1½ tons. It contained 573 lb flour; 382 lb raisins; 191 lb currants; 191 lb bread; 382 lb suet; a 'great number of eggs'; 360 quarts of milk; 320 lemons; 95 lb sugar and 144 nutmegs. It cost nearly £50 and the pudding was drawn by eight horses to the green, where the public dinner took place.

The line was extended to Brixham Road for passengers on 14 March 1861 and for freight a fortnight later on 1 April. The intention had been for the line to cross the river near Dittisham Ferry and terminate at Dartmouth, but a landowner successfully objected. Passenger traffic opened to a terminus at Kingswear, 13¾ miles from Aller Junction, on 16 August 1864 and to goods on 2 April 1866. The £90,000 estimated cost of the line proved to be inaccurate, actual expenses being £262,000. The SDR, the working company, absorbed the line in 1872. The branch was converted to standard gauge between 20 and 23 May 1892.

South of Paignton the railway was formally closed by BR in October 1972, the Dart Valley Railway taking over the line as the Torbay Steam Railway. Since it was impossible to share BR's station at Paignton, a new station, Queen's Park, was constructed alongside in 1973 on what used to be BR's Down carriage sidings. The Up carriage sidings were retained by BR for stabling and reversal purposes. When it was decided that the Buckfastleigh line should become independent, the Torbay Steam Railway changed its name to the Paignton & Dartmouth Steam Railway.

The Torbay line originally started from its own station at Newton Abbot and ran parallel with the Plymouth line to Aller. Unusually the main line curves away from the branch. The Plymouth line was also single and in 1855 a junction was laid at Aller, the two parallel roads becoming the Up and Down lines. On 1 July 1874 the junction was abolished and the branch extended to Newton Abbot as an independent third line, while

The ceremony of turning the first turf of the Dartmouth & Torbay Railway, Torquay.
21.1.1858 Courtesy: *Illustrated London News*

a couple of years later it was doubled to Kingskerswell. A 50 m.p.h. speed restriction was imposed at Aller Junction and on the rest of the branch to Kingswear. Beyond the junction the branch rises at 1 in 162 and steepens to 1 in 110 for 2 miles past Kingskerswell, opened in 1853, to the summit. This station closed to goods on 5 August 1963 and to passengers on 5 October 1964. The line then descends at 1 in 72 to Torre, named Torquay until 2 August 1859. This has a Grade II listed timber building of Italianate design, now an antique shop, on the Down platform and an unusual three-storey signal-box on the Up. Torre had a large, stone-built goods shed and, until closure to freight on 4 December 1967, was the railhead for Torquay, no goods facilities being provided at Torquay station. As the gradient steepens to 1 in 55 to Torquay, stringent rules applied to guard against runaways while shunting. No less than six sprags had to be kept 10 yd apart in the six-foot between the points of the Down refuge siding and Stop Board, and the same number between the passenger platforms at the Torquay end of the station. The layout at Torre, as at Torquay and Paignton, allowed the Up platform to be used by Down trains for arrival and departure. This assisted working at times of peak summer Saturday traffic.

The present Torquay station, a delightful building of French pavilion type with a cast-iron crest to its roof, opened in 1873 replacing an earlier structure. Both platforms have an attractive arcade with decorative canopy support columns imaginatively painted to bring out their features. Pleasant gardens are situated on both platforms. The railway was mainly responsible for the town's population increasing from 5,982 in 1841 to 21,657 in 1871.

When the signalman was unable to observe the tail lamp of an Up train, either due to its length or because his view was obstructed by a Down train, he had to ascertain from a responsible member of the station staff that the Up train was complete with tail lamp.

Cover of GWR Public Notice concerning the conversion from broad to standard gauge 1892.

Torquay station used to be very busy on summer Saturdays – the total arrivals for all Saturdays from 22 June until 14 September 1957 was 94,464 passengers originating from: London (40 per cent), the North-West (17 per cent), the Midlands (15½ per cent), the North (15 per cent), Bristol (6½ per cent) and South Wales (6 per cent). Incoming visitors started arriving early – the 9.12 p.m. Fridays-only from Nottingham was due at 4.30 a.m. Even though no freight trains ran on the branch on summer Saturdays and some local trains were cancelled, seat regulation had to be enforced on Friday nights and Saturdays from mid-June until mid-September, passengers being required to purchase a travel ticket in advance and obtain a free regulation ticket entitling them to a seat. When all regulation tickets for a certain train were issued, passengers were offered seats on an alternative service.

Number of passengers arriving on the fourteen busiest summer Saturdays:

	1956	1962
Torquay and Torre	98,042	76,252
Paignton	70,365	59,928

Down trains leaving Torquay pass below an attractive overbridge, its decorations picked out in green, red and gold. They climb briefly at 1 in 57 to the Gas Works summit. Livermead, or Torquay, tunnel, 133 yd in length, was opened out when the track was doubled to Paignton on 30 October 1910, though a landslide two months later caused the line to revert to single track for a few weeks. This was not the first slip, for in 1903 a landslide between the gasworks and tunnel caused the line to be relaid further inland.

Normally Gas House siding signal-box was only in circuit to work the sidings, but on summer Saturdays it was manned from 6.00 a.m. till 6.00 p.m. to create a shorter section. The sidings were in use from 1892 till 1969.

Preston Platform, just beyond Gas House siding, opened on 24 July 1911 almost coinciding with the withdrawal of the GWR bus service between Paignton and Torquay, which had started on 11 July 1904. The new platform served the nearby promenade and residential area. Preston Platform closed on 21 September 1914. The line falls at 1 in 81 to Paignton where the Up platform is signalled for Up and Down working. The station premises compare unfavourably with those at Torquay.

Single track existed beyond the station until 1931 when the GWR used available government funds to make extensive capital improvements, the implementation of which also helped to relieve unemployment. Double track was extended a further ½ mile to Goodrington Sands, and extra carriage sidings and an extensive goods depot were laid alongside, the latter closing on 4 December 1967. When this new goods depot opened, the old goods shed was used for 'Passengers Luggage in Advance' for the Torbay area. In 1930 the number of staff employed at Paignton was forty, with an additional eight in the summer.

For the first fifteen years Paignton & Dartmouth Steam Railway trains were signalled out of Queen's Park station by a BR signalman at Paignton South signal-box, but since 1987 when BR re-signalled its own line, PDSR locomotive crews have operated the crossing controls for Sands Road, south of the station.

Goodrington Sands halt, opened 9 July 1928, was simply Goodrington until 24 September 1928. The single track through the station was doubled and a Down platform opened on 4 July 1930. Some trains were scheduled to terminate or start from here, inclusive of summer season trains from and to Saltash or Plymouth, Moretonhampstead and Swansea or Cardiff.

Between Goodrington and Kingswear the line is very scenic: firstly coastal over Torbay and later with views of the River Dart and Dartmouth. There is a 2 mile climb at 1 in 71/60 to Churston, passing en route the 73 yd long Broadsands Viaduct; Broadsands halt was opened on 9 July 1928 and used until 23 September 1929, but only by excursions. Hookhills Viaduct, 27 chains to the south, is 148 yd long.

There was a passing loop at Churston and a bay platform for Brixham trains. When Churston was the terminus of the branch from Newton Abbot, a turntable and engine shed were provided south of the platform. Today the PDSR has a locomotive service depot at Churston. On 20 October 1968 BR took out the passing loop, but this was restored by the preservationists in 1979.

The line descends at 1 in 75 to Greenway Tunnel, 495 yd, through which the gradient eases to 1 in 100 and then steepens to 1½ miles of 1 in 66 to Kingswear Crossing halt. It is very dramatic emerging from the tunnel, crossing the curving Greenway Viaduct with superb views across and along the Dart below. The line originally crossed Longwood and Noss Creeks by timber viaducts, but on 20 May 1923 the line was re-routed around these inlets.

Kingswear Crossing halt, first used in 1877, was later renamed Steam Ferry Crossing halt and then Britannia halt, but did not appear in the public timetables, the four trains calling for the benefit of naval personnel and shipbuilders across the river. In 1990 to cope with the heavy summer traffic, electric colour light signalling was installed along the 6½ mile length of the PDSR and controlled from a new signal-box at Britannia Crossing.

The track is level to Kingswear and formerly a ticket platform was sited on the Down side at the station throat. The passenger platform has two faces, one partly covered by

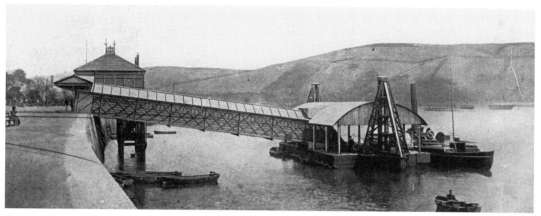

Pontoon landing stage and approach to the GWR's trackless station at Dartmouth.

c. 1905 Author's collection

the train shed. One station approach is through an arch beneath the Royal Dart Hotel. The floating pontoon beyond the station led to the former railway-owned ferry. The engine shed closed on 14 July 1924 and latterly provision was merely an engine road with turntable. Kingswear also had a cattle dock, five short carriage sidings, the longest holding eight coaches. The quayside sidings were principally for coal arriving by sea for Torquay gasworks, this traffic lasting till about 1950. The coal wharf is now Dart Haven Marina car park.

One of the GWR's claims for being different was that for eighty-seven years it had a station to which no rails were ever laid. Dartmouth station has a fine cast-iron crest to its slate roof, and a glazed and valanced canopy on its road side. The pontoons were roofed with corrugated iron. It was not directly opposite Kingswear, but several hundred yards up river. Due to the Royal Naval College traffic, for many years the station-master at Dartmouth was of a higher grade than his colleague at Kingswear – despite not having any trains!

For the first few years the Dartmouth Steam Packet Company worked the ferry on behalf of the SDR using the PS *Perseverance* from 1864–9, followed by the PS *Dolphin* using *Perseverance*'s boiler and engine. This had bows at each end and drop rudders enabling it to steam in either direction – in fact it was a marine version of an auto-train! SS *The Mew* built at Falmouth by Messrs Cox, worked from 20 May 1908 until 8 October 1954. Licensed to carry 543 passengers, in 1924 it was modified to carry two lorries or four cars. GWR delivery lorries were ferried across, and there were specially busy sailings at the beginning and end of the Royal Naval College terms. Although sent to Dover at the time of the Dunkirk evacuation, *The Mew* was not used as its draught was too great to get close to the beach and she was too small to carry large numbers from offshore. From 1954 BR used a motor launch for two and a half years until it was replaced by two new diesel-powered ferries, *Adrian Gilbert* and *Humphrey Gilbert*, which lasted until 1972 when the ferry was taken over by the local authority. In 1976 a private operator bought the ferry.

The train service in 1887 offered eleven from Newton Abbot to Kingswear, with three on Sundays, the time taken being about 60 minutes. In 1910 fifteen were run on weekdays and six on Sundays, the journey time being decreased to about 55 minutes. In

Dartmouth station and a solid-tyred GWR parcels delivery van.

c. 1920 Author's collection

1938 the service had been increased further to twenty-three on weekdays and nine on Sundays. In 1960 there were seventeen Down and eighteen Up Mondays to Fridays; seventeen Down and fifteen Up on Saturdays, and nine each way on Sundays. In 1994, Newton Abbot to Paignton, twenty-seven Down and thirty Up trains are shown on weekdays, twenty-nine and thirty respectively on Saturdays and nineteen each way on Sundays.

The branch was one of the very few on which 'Kings' and 47XX class 2–8–0s could run and so most GWR types appeared on the line at one time or another.

Pride of place in the PDSR motive power shed is held jointly by No. 4920 *Dumbleton Hall* and No. 7827 *Lydham Manor*, but the most powerful is 2–8–0T No. 5239, now named *Goliath*. Other locomotives are 2–6–2Ts No. 4555 and No. 4588; 0–6–0PTs No. 1638 and No. 6435; Class 03 D2192; Class 08 D3014 and Class 25 D7535 *Mercury*.

The 'Devon Belle' observation car has a chassis built in 1917 by the LNWR as an ambulance car, and was given a Pullman body in 1921. It was rebuilt after the Second World War with an observation end for the SR's 'Devon Belle' running between Waterloo and Ilfracombe, and later ran under BR from Inverness to the Kyle of Lochalsh.

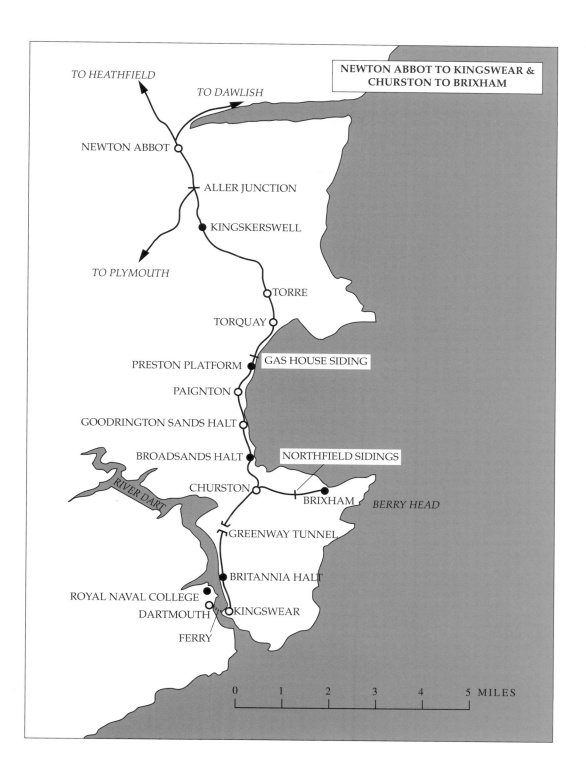

55XX class 2–6–2T No. 5557 on arrival at Newton Abbot working the 6.15 p.m. branch train from Kingswear.

c. 1937 E.J.M. Hayward

Sprinter 150249 at Aller Junction with the 08.54 Exeter, St David's to Paignton. The double tracks for the main line and branch are now independent at this point and to the south end of Newton Abbot station.

31.5.94 Author

Express 158865 leaving Torquay with the 08.00 Cardiff to Paignton.

31.5.94 Author

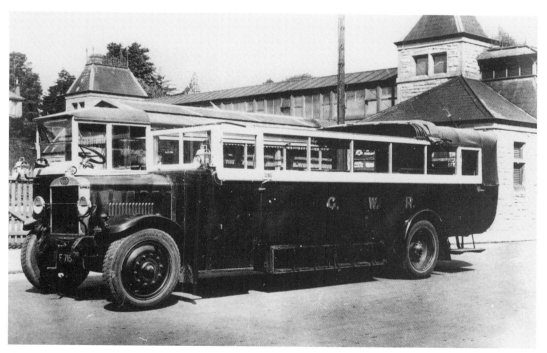

GWR bus No. 1280, registration YF 715, at Torquay station. First licensed on 21 March 1927, it has a Guy chassis and Buckingham 32-seat body.

c. 1928 Author's collection

No. 4079 *Pendennis Castle* passing Gas House siding with a Cardiff to Paignton excursion. No. 4079 is preserved in Australia.

Easter Sunday 1937 E.J.M. Hayward

Semi-streamlined No. 6014 *King Henry VII* approaches Paignton North level-crossing with the Down Torbay Express.

Easter 1937 E.J.M. Hayward

24 hp Straker-Squire Fleet No. 78, registration AF 161, at Paignton having worked the GWR bus service from Torquay. This route commenced on 2 April 1906.

c. 1906 Author's collection

45XX class 2–6–2T No. 4588 at Goodrington on the preserved line.

June 1973 R.E. Toop

No. 5064 *Bishop's Castle* crossing Hookhills Viaduct with a Paddington to Kingswear train. A fogman's hut is at the foot of the Fixed Distant signal.

13.8.55 R.E. Toop

Churston, view Down showing the engine shed with D2192 *Ardent* and 45XX class 2–6–2T No. 4588 outside.

31.5.94 Author

45XX class 2–6–2T No. 4582 ascending to Churston with coal from Kingswear to Torquay gasworks.

27.7.53 R.E. Toop

North of Britannia halt a passenger train hauled by a 45XX class 2–6–2T takes the old line across Longwood timber viaduct, while the diversion, yet to be opened, is in the foreground.

c. 1922 Author's collection

113

A GWR horse-drawn parcels delivery van and another vehicle crossing the River Dart.

c. 1920 Author's collection

No. 6018 *King Henry VI* heads an Up Torbay Express at Kingswear.

c. 1936 E.J.M. Hayward

4–4–0 No. 3440 *City of Truro* and 2–6–2T head a special at Kingswear.

19.5.57 M.E.J. Deane

Kingswear station. This photograph is taken from almost the same viewpoint as the one shown opposite.

31.5.94 Author

Churston to Brixham

The 2 mile long Churston to Brixham branch was unusual in that it was built solely through the efforts of one man, R.W. Wolston of Brixham. On 25 July 1864 an Act of Parliament was granted for building the Torbay & Brixham Railway. Of the £18,000 capital, Wolston held £17,700 worth of shares, the remaining £300 being taken by two relatives and one of Wolston's friends.

When the contractor defaulted, Wolston superintended the line's completion. The single broad gauge branch opened to passengers on 28 February 1868 and to goods on 1 May. Wolston purchased the 0–4–0WT *Queen*, which had been used for building Portland Breakwater, rolling stock being hired from the SDR, which worked the branch.

Although the line carried a considerable volume of fish traffic in addition to the ordinary traffic found on a branch line, the books failed to balance and in July 1870 Wolston mortgaged his engine as security. When almost bankrupt, some friends engaged an experienced railway accountant to examine the balance sheet and it was discovered that the SDR had failed to credit the Torbay & Brixham with the terminal charges to which it was entitled. The SDR disagreed with these findings so the TBR appealed to the Railway & Canal Commissioners. At a hearing in July 1876 they decided in favour of the TBR. The SDR did not accept defeat graciously, but introduced an exorbitant charge for the use of Churston station. The TBR made a further appeal to the Commissioners who, in March 1877, again upheld the TBR and forced the SDR to pay the Brixham company £2,000.

On 1 February 1876, while this litigation was in progress, the GWR had taken over the SDR and worked the Brixham branch with GWR rolling stock and *Queen*, supplying a replacement locomotive when she required maintenance. In January 1877 the GWR sold the ex-SDR 0–4–0T *Raven* to the TBR, the engine retaining its GWR numberplate 2175. It was converted to standard gauge in August 1892, purchased by the Wantage Tramway in 1910 and cut up after a collision in 1919.

The Torbay & Brixham Railway was sold to the GWR for £12,000 on 1 January 1883 and converted to standard gauge on 20–3 May 1892. A fuel crisis early in 1951 closed the line temporarily and the branch finally shut to passengers and goods on 13 August 1963.

Only just over 2 miles in length, the branch was one of the shortest on the GWR. Trains started from the bay platform at Churston, with its own small waiting shelter at the Up end of the Down main platform. Although during the twenties and thirties an auto-coach, or at the most two, was worked by a 2–4–0T or 0–4–2T, on Sundays three- and four-coach trains, some working through from Newton Abbot, Exeter and Taunton, were run headed by 45XX class 2–6–2Ts, even though the Churston bay platform could not accommodate such a length.

From Churston the line rose at 1 in 95 for just over 1¼ miles and then fell at 1 in 78 to Brixham, the station situated inconveniently above the town. About ½ mile west of the terminus were the Air Ministry's Northfield sidings, opened on 23 October 1940 and later used by the Ministry of Power.

Brixham station building was constructed of timber, the GWR adding a standard platform awning, probably in 1894 when the platforms were lengthened at both ends. East of the passenger station was the goods shed with the fish shed opposite. In 1925 a daily average of six coal wagons were received, one wagon of general goods forwarded and thirteen received. Fish was important and left by train almost daily until the line's closure. In 1957 1,000 tons of fish were despatched averaging three to five vans daily. On Sundays the branch could be specially opened for fish traffic as long as a minimum of 5 tons of fish were required to be carried.

Certain passenger services were allowed to be worked without a guard, although restrictions stated that they should not exceed three eight-wheel vehicles, or two coaches and two four-wheeled vehicles, or one coach and three four-wheeled vehicles. The station staff were required to see that all doors were properly closed and all luggage, mail and parcels were locked in the luggage bodies inaccessible to passengers. The fireman was responsible for obtaining the wooden staff from, and taking it to, the signalman at Churston.

Another regulation stated that at Brixham the gravitation of vehicles was prohibited unless absolutely necessary, and six sprags, 10 yd apart, were to be kept between the main line and the sidings. A train to Northfield sidings was not to exceed sixteen tank wagons, and to guard against runaways, a train working the siding was to be in the loop line with not less than six sprags kept alongside.

The timber-built engine shed, opened in February 1868, was pulled down in 1896, its corrugated iron replacement being opened in 1897 and closed on 22 July 1929.

Until the branch's last days the timetable showed an increasing frequency. In 1887 there were eight Down and ten Up trains with three each way on Sundays; in 1910 thirteen ran each way and on Sunday seven Down and five Up. By 1922 seventeen ran on weekdays but none on Sundays, while in 1938 no less than twenty-five ran on weekdays and seven on Sundays. In 1960 twelve ran each way on weekdays plus an additional five on Saturdays.

4–4–0ST No. 13 at Churston with a train for Brixham. A fish and poultry wagon, the body of which is mounted on an ex-broad gauge carriage underframe, is next to the engine. No. 13 was a 'one-off', built in 1886 as a 2–4–2WT and altered in 1897 to the form depicted. She was withdrawn in May 1926.

c. 1905 Author's collection

A four-coach train being pushed out from the Brixham bay at Churston so that the 45XX class 2–6–2T can run round.

c. 1930 Lens of Sutton

14XX 0–4–2T No. 1427 at Churston heads auto-trailer W222W to Brixham, while a Down stopping train to Kingswear arrives behind No. 1010 *County of Caernarvon*.

8.8.55 R.E. Toop

Now preserved at Didcot, 14XX class 0–4–2T No. 1466 propels its one coach auto-train from Churston.

6.8.53 R.E. Toop

An 0–6–0ST at Brixham. The bridge rail is on longitudinal sleepers. Note that a rather out-of-scale standard GWR canopy has been erected in front of the original low building.

c. 1905 Author's collection

14XX class 0–4–2T No. 1452 at Brixham with a two-coach train.

c. 1960 Lens of Sutton

55XX class 2–6–2T No. 5573 of 83A (Newton Abbot) at Brixham with a permanent way train.

7.8.60 R.E. Toop

A single-car DMU at Brixham.

c. 1963 Lens of Sutton

Totnes to Ashburton

The 9½ mile long Buckfastleigh, Totnes and South Devon Railway was authorized on 25 June 1864, while a further Act of 26 May 1865 allowed an extension to be built to Ashburton. The first sod was cut at Buckfastleigh on 3 August 1865, but by the end of 1867 work had stopped pending negotiations with the contractor, the result being that another was appointed the following year.

The line opened on 1 May 1872, was worked by the SDR, and converted to standard gauge in 1892. A special train left Chester at midnight on 19 May with 441 permanent way men, picking up en route 168 from Swindon Works, arrived at Ashburton at 2.40 p.m. A special train of empty broad gauge passenger stock left Ashburton at 10.00 p.m. on Friday 20 May. The branch was then converted and on Monday a standard gauge six-wheel first- and second-class compo and two brake thirds arrived to form the new branch train and at 6.30 a.m. on Tuesday 24 May a narrow gauge special was run to return the workmen to their homes. The Buckfastleigh line was purchased by the GWR on 28 August 1897.

To reach Newton Abbot, the main commercial centre for Ashburton, involved a change of train at Totnes, the trip taking more than twice as long as a bus which completed the journey in 25 minutes. The branch closed to passengers on 1 November 1958, 0–4–2Ts Nos 1466 and 1470 working the last train. Goods services were withdrawn on 7 September 1962.

The line was taken over for preservation by the Dart Valley Light Railway and on 5 April 1969 the first public passenger train for eleven years ran from Buckfastleigh to Totnes. On 21 May 1969 the line was officially reopened by Dr Richard Beeching, the man responsible for closing so many of Britain's branch lines. Since 1971 the terminus had to be cut back to Buckfastleigh as the new A38 required some of the land. The DVLR's headquarters were established at Buckfastleigh where there is now a workshop, engine shed and 10 acres of riverside grounds forming a park.

For many years Totnes Riverside was the southern terminus of the preserved line. Passengers were unable to leave the railway and walk to Totnes as there was no public access. From Easter 1985 the DVLR started to work in and out of BR Totnes, then in 1988 BR safety regulations required DVLR locomotives and stock using its station to be maintained to main line, and not light railway, standards. The cost of this would have been prohibitive, so trains were again cut back to DVLR's Riverside station, renamed Littlehempston in which parish it stood. The station building came from Toller on the Bridport branch. At present only one platform face is used, but provision is made for a second platform road to be laid. An important improvement was a footbridge, opened on 30 September 1993, giving access to the BR station and the town.

In 1989 the railway's support association took over the running of the line. The Dumbleton Hall Locomotive Trust leased the branch on 1 January 1991, but as the terms forbade the use

TIME TABLES OF SPECIAL EMPTY B.G. PASSENGER TRAINS TO SWINDON, FRIDAY, MAY 20TH.

Special Trains will run from the West of England to Swindon as follows, for the purpose of clearing the Line West of Exeter of all Broad Gauge Passenger Stock.

NOTE.—Before the Coaches are sent away the Stations should be careful to take out all lamps and take off all label boards, spare screw couplings, &c.

FROM ASHBURTON BRANCH.

FRIDAY, MAY 20th.

ASHBURTON TO TOTNES.		arr. p.m.	dep. p.m.	TOTNES TO SWINDON.			arr. p.m.	dep. p.m.
Ashburton	.. .. ..	—	10 0	Totnes	.. .. ..	—	10 45
Buckfastleigh	.. .. ..	10 6	10 10	Newton Abbot	.. ..	11 10	11 20
Staverton	.. .. ..	10 16	10 20	Exeter	(SAT. MORNING)	12 5	12 15
Totnes	.. .. ..	10 30	—	Taunton	.. ..	1 30	1 40
				Bristol	.. ..	3 30	3 40
				Bath	.. .. pass	4 7	
				Chippenham	.. ..	4 37	4 45
				Swindon F. Cabin	.. ..	5 20	a.m.

Information from an official booklet giving details of clearing broad gauge stock before Gauge Conversion and timetable of workmen's trains, 1892.

of the words 'Dart' and 'Valley' in the title, the name of South Devon Railway was resurrected. With this reorganization, some of the engines which had worked on the DVLR were transferred to the Paignton to Kingswear line. Hitherto the branch had a 16 ton axle limit, but bridges were strengthened to allow 28XX class No. 3803 to work the line.

Totnes main line station had four through tracks, those serving the platforms being the outer roads. Rather unusually, there was no bay platform for the branch train. This meant that Ashburton trains could only use the platforms when no other trains were signalled – connections were consequently poor. Branch trains crossed the River Dart to Ashburton Junction where the lines diverged, the double track soon becoming single.

Staverton had one platform on the north side of the line and a solitary goods siding. Near Stretchford and GWR provided a siding for the transport of iron ore to Totnes Quay, ore being brought from mines the other side of the river by a narrow gauge horse-worked line.

Buckfastleigh had two platforms, the Down considerably longer than the Up and a goods shed adjoining the Down platform. The loop was lengthened on 23 December 1906.

The line passed through the 47 yd long Gulwell Tunnel just before Ashburton, where the passenger station was of the train shed variety and almost identical to that previously constructed at Moretonhampstead. The station also had a goods shed and cattle pen. The gasworks closed just prior to the Second World War, its coal being unloaded in the goods yard and taken onwards by horse and cart. When the wool mills were working at full capacity, Buckfastleigh's goods revenue exceeded that of any of the SDR's main line stations.

Four main cattle fairs were held at Ashburton and each required up to ninety trucks. Since the yard had insufficient capacity, some were stored at Buckfastleigh. All day a locomotive was employed to take wagons the 2½ miles from Buckfastleigh to Ashburton and back; they were held at Buckfastleigh until there were sufficient for a trip to Totnes. Initially these cattle workings were fitted between passenger trains, but latterly passenger trains on fair days ran only to Buckfastleigh, a bus making the final leg to the terminus.

One of the first engines used on the branch was SDR 0–6–0ST *Taurus*, also 'Hawthorn' class 2–4–0STs *Melling* and *Bury*, and the 2–4–0T 'Metropolitan' class *Cerberus*. In standard gauge days 517 class 0–4–2Ts, Metro 2–4–0Ts worked passenger trains, while 44XX or 45XX 2–6–2Ts appeared on goods trains. In later years 14XX class 0–4–2Ts were used and occasionally 16XX class 0–6–0PTs. 0–4–2T No. 1470, known locally as Bulliver, worked the branch for many years. Its name was probably a corruption of Bolivar, for in Kipling's *Ballad of Bolivar* one verse reads:

> Rocketing, her rivets loose, smoke stark white as snow,
> All the coals adrift adeck, half the rails below,
> Looking like a lobster pot, steering like a dray –
> Out we took the 'Boliver', out across the Bay.

Locomotives normally faced the terminus, but following the introduction of auto-coaches around 1930 they faced the Up direction and propelled the coaches to Ashburton. On two evenings in October 1947 No. 5094 *Tretower Castle* worked the Royal train to a point between Totnes and Staverton, where it spent the night.

A ganger's tricycle in the railway museum at Buckfastleigh. Used on many GWR branch lines, these were propelled by rocking the handle backwards and forwards.

31.5.94 Author

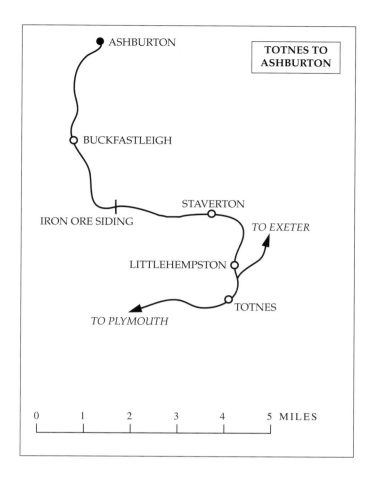

The engine shed at Ashburton had stone walls and a slate roof; it closed when the passenger service was withdrawn. Until about 1930 an overnight cleaner coaled the engine, raked the ashpan, cleaned the engine, and before the driver arrived next morning, built up the fire and pumped water into the tank. Post-1930 the early fireman lit, or built up, the fire, pumped water and carried out the cleaning duties.

The train service remained stable throughout the life of the branch, with six or seven trains, each way taking about 28 minutes in 1887 and 22 in 1957. Speed was limited to 40 m.p.h.

Present SDR stock includes:

Class	Wheel arrangement	No.
14XX	0–4–2T	1420
1366	0–6–0PT	1369
57XX	0–6–0PT	5786
57XX	0–6–0PT	7714
45XX	2–6–2T	5526
BR Standard Class 4	2–6–4T	80064
WD	0–6–0ST	68011 *Errol Lonsdale*

Totnes station sign. This picture was taken when the station won the GWR Best Kept Station competition.

1926 Author's collection

517 class 0–4–2T No. 1163 at Totnes with auto-trailer No. 130 newly painted in 1930 livery. It was ex-steam rail motor No. 33.

c. 1932 Lens of Sutton

Plate on the footbridge across the River Dart linking the BR and SDR stations, Totnes.

31.5.94 Author

16XX class 0–6–0PT No. 1638 near Staverton.

17.8.71 R.E. Toop

Staverton, view Down.

c. 1920 Author's collection

Staverton, view Down. This photograph was taken from almost the same viewpoint as the one above.

31.5.94 Author

A 517 class 0–4–2T and three four-wheeled coaches with an Up train at Buckfastleigh. Notice the burnished buffers. Posters advertise GWR hotels and trips to London, Reading, Dublin and the Channel Islands.

c. 1908 Lens of Sutton

14XX class 0–4–2T No. 1470 on the last day of passenger service at Buckfastleigh.

1.1.58 Author's collection

Frontage of Ashburton station.

c. 1910 Author's collection

Frontage of the former Ashburton terminus, now the Station Garage.

31.5.94 Author

Track on longitudinal sleepers at Ashburton. View to terminus.

c. 1900 Lens of Sutton

View of Ashburton station from the buffers. Two wagons of locomotive coal stand on the left. The van in the background is at the cattle dock.

c. 1932 Lens of Sutton

A 44XX class 2–6–2T at Ashburton. The engine shed can be seen in the distance.

c. 1958 M.E.J. Deane

14XX class 0–4–2T No. 1470 shunting cattle wagons at Ashburton. The photographer was standing in front of the locomotive shed which explains the ash and clinker in the foreground.

c. 1961 M.E.J. Deane

The Industrial Branches

The Westleigh Tramway

The Westleigh Quarries, leased by a group led by J.C. Wall, general manager of the Bristol & Exeter Railway, made an agreement with the B&E to work its line for twenty-five years from March 1873. The Westleigh Tramway's engineer was Arthur Cadlick Pain, who held the same post with the nearby Culm Valley Railway. As the gauge was 3 ft, the stone had to be transhipped at Burlescombe into broad gauge wagons.

The tramway, just over ½ mile in length, opened on 12 January 1875 and was the last addition to the B&E before amalgamation with the GWR the following year. The B&E had three gauges and in this respect was probably unique at that time. Two locomotives were specially built at the B&E's Bristol Works. These 0–4–0WTs had 2 ft diameter wheels and a 5 ft 3 in wheelbase.

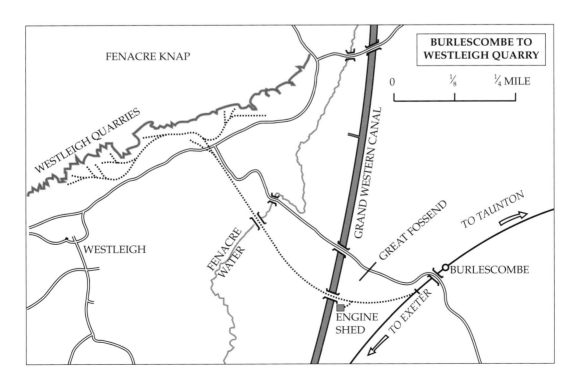

133

B&E No.	Date Built	GWR No.	Withdrawn	
112	January 1874	1381	1.1899	
113	August 1875	1382	1.1899	Sold to Manchester Corporation Rivers Dept at Davyhulme, named *Bear* and scrapped 1914.

When these engines were taken over by the GWR a brass number plate was fixed to the back of the cab, there being no suitable surface on the side. The locomotive shed, sited immediately west of the cattle dock at Burlescombe, had timber walls and a slate roof. It closed in October 1898.

When the B&E's lease expired the quarry company converted the line to standard gauge and worked the line itself. It laid Vignoles rail, spiked directly to the sleepers, but sidings and points were of bridge rail on cross sleepers and remained intact when rail traffic ceased about 1950. The connection with the main line was severed in January 1961. In 1977 some trackwork still remained at the Burlescombe end and its owners, English China Clays, allowed lifting and transfer to the Great Western Society at Didcot where it was relaid as a mixed gauge line.

Standard gauge locomotives used on the tramway:

Name	Wheel arrangement	Maker	Maker's No.	Date	Notes
Cantreff	0–6–0ST	Manning Wardle	1235	1893	Purchased from Cardiff Corporation Water Works *c.* 1900. In 1926 sold in part-exchange for Peckett 1717. To Byfield Ironstone Co. Ltd., Northants, June 1929. Scrapped 1963.
–	0–6–0ST	Peckett	1717	1926	Scrapped December 1954

The standard gauge engine was kept in a timber shed at ground level on the south side of the Grand Western Canal and had to climb 1 in 25 to the main line of the tramway. On the embankment was a large water tank. The driver lived adjacent to the shed and quadrupled as fireman, shunter and permanent way man. Most of the traffic was carried in the company's own wagons and in 1950 the engine was steamed no more than thrice weekly.

The ¾ mile long branch had considerable engineering works for an industrial line. In narrow gauge days, light timber trestles carried the line over a valley and the Grand Western Canal, but the standard gauge line had embankments about 20 ft high and a steel girder bridge across the canal. The embankment slopes are now tree-covered and two brick overbridges near Cracker Corner at the quarry end of the line can still be seen.

Some 150 yd from Burlescombe station the line crossed the canal and occupation road by a bridge whose two spans total 80 ft and which is still extant. About 200 yd beyond, the descent at 1 in 40 changed to a rise of 1 in 50 towards the quarry.

Exeter City Basin Branch

Powers for building the 750 yd long City Basin line were obtained in the SDR's Act of 5 July 1865. Of mixed gauge it was to be completed within two years. Tenders were not considered until 14 June 1866 and that of J. Barow, Newton Abbot, was accepted at £633 14s 2d. Earthworks and ballasting were completed in February 1867 and the line opened on 17 June 1867. Just broad gauge at first, wagon turntables gave access to three sides of the basin. In February 1870 a third rail was added and by the autumn the main line from Exeter, St David's to City Basin Junction had been converted to mixed gauge, but no connection was made with the Up main line. The standard gauge remained useless as there was no outlet until 20 March 1871 when a link was made with the standard gauge LSWR. The gasworks siding opened in January 1875, a fact which must have galled Exeter Corporation, owners of the basin, as the gas company had purposely established the works there so that coal could be brought by water.

The GWR refused to work the standard gauge line, though until 1 March 1876 this would have been uneconomic as the GWR's mixed gauge did not reach Exeter until that date: this meant that goods consigned by LSWR had to travel from the Basin to St David's in broad gauge trucks at 6d a ton and pay a further 9d for transfer to standard

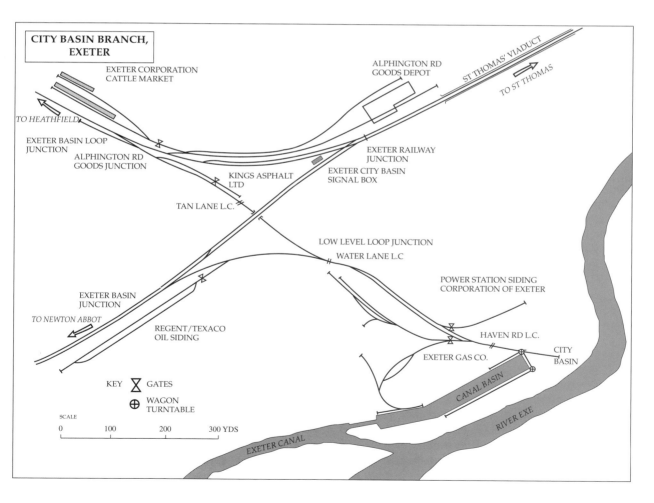

gauge wagon before starting on the LSWR. The GWR began working standard gauge traffic to the Basin in October 1876.

The City Basin train consisted of both broad and standard gauge wagons linked by a match truck with especially wide buffers to be suitable for buffers of both gauges. The coupling chain at each end slid on a transverse bar.

Traffic from ship to rail did not develop as anticipated and in 1883 such tonnage carried by the branch was only 389 outwards and 30 inwards. In 1962 the Basin line handled 54,762 tons of freight, 53,066 being 'motor spirit'. The branch closed to public traffic in September 1965, becoming just a private siding to the Texaco oil depot and the gasworks.

The gasworks siding used horse traction until 1903, but from this date until closure in 1971 five steam and two diesel locomotives were used at different times. Although most coal arrived by rail, some came by sea and locomotives were used for the short haul between Basin and gasworks.

Ten to twenty oil-tank wagons from Avonmouth arrived on three to four days each week and were returned empty the same day. Rail deliveries ceased about 1979 and the siding closed on 21 July 1983. King's Asphalt was another user of the line.

At first no signalling was provided at Exeter Basin Junction which meant that a Down goods working the Basin branch could not be shut in to allow the passage of another Down train on the main line. In 1902 the branch points, instead of being worked from a ground frame, were operated from the new City Basin Junction box built for the opening of the Exeter Railway.

A restriction on the type of locomotive and the weight of the train meant that for many years a 44XX class 2–6–2T was shedded at Exeter specially for working the branch.

The Teignmouth Quay Branch

Around 1850 a private siding was laid from the main line to the Old Quay, about ¼ mile west of Teignmouth station. In September 1886 the Teignmouth Quay Company Limited was formed to take over the Old Quay and expand it. A new connection was put in with the main line, the Quay Company paying the cost of a new signal-box, opened in 1894, the previous connection having been worked from a ground frame. The Quay Company also paid £40 a year towards the signalman's wages, this sum being about two-thirds of the total. In the 1900s coal arrived by sea and was despatched by rail, as was timber and wood pulp, these going to Cullompton and Hele. Clay arrived by rail and left by sea. In the 1930s the quays and facilities for handling the coal and clay traffic were modernized. From 1931 slack coal was imported for the new Newton Abbot power-station and was forwarded by rail.

In the early years the signal-box was in circuit weekdays from 8.00 a.m. till 6.00 p.m. and one train shunted daily. From 1928 till the 1950s the three shunts daily declined to two and then one until 2 December 1967, when the private siding agreement was terminated due to the opening of the Exmouth Junction Coal Concentration Depot. The clay traffic from North Devon and Wareham, which had come by rail, was now lost by Teignmouth.

Wagons were allowed to be propelled from Teignmouth to Old Quay in clear weather and during daylight hours, but this trip was not to be carried out when a passenger train was signalled on the Up line. A brake van was not required, but a shunter was required to walk beside, or ride, in the leading vehicle.

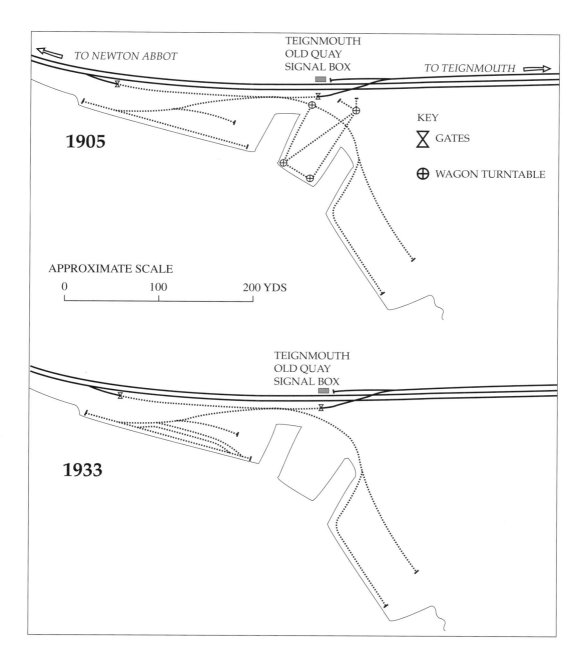

TEIGNMOUTH
OLD QUAY
SIGNAL BOX

TO TEIGNMOUTH

1905

KEY

✕ GATES

⊕ WAGON TURNTABLE

APPROXIMATE SCALE

0   100   200 YDS

TEIGNMOUTH
OLD QUAY
SIGNAL BOX

1933

Locomotives were not permitted beyond the Stop Board just inside the gate to the quay. Shunting on the Quay Company's track was initially performed by horses. These animals were so skilful that they could draw a wagon and turn it 90° on a turntable and onwards without stopping, a feat which was to their advantage as great energy was required when starting a wagon from rest. About 1920 a petrol tractor replaced horses, but proved inadequate. A Sentinel steam road tractor, Works No. 5644, built in 1924 and purchased about 1931, was fitted with timber baulks to act as buffers. Named *The Elephant*, (the company's name on the roof valence was picked out in Crown bottle caps), it worked until 1963 and is now preserved. One siding which *The Elephant* could not work due to limited clearance, or lack of suitable road surface, had electrically-powered capstans for moving wagons. From 1963 until 1967 a farm diesel tractor fitted with baulks was used.

The Totnes Quay Branch

The ¾ mile long Totnes Quay branch opened on 10 November 1873 as part of the Buckfastleigh, Totnes and South Devon Railway.

It branched from a siding off the Down main line just east of Totnes station and curved sharply southwards, crossing the Mill Leat near the racecourse. Just beyond was the River Dart siding, also known as Totnes Racecourse siding and opened as late as 1944, which trailed in from Totnes Market and South Devon Farmers. A short distance further on, the loop siding added about 1914 ended at Tram Gate and just beyond was a facing siding removed in September 1964. The line recrossed Mill Leat and ended at Marsh Quay, where Mill Leat widened into Mill Tail. Symonds Cyder had premises here and nearby was a crane and railway wagon weighbridge. Timber was imported at Totnes Quay and loaded directly from riverside storage sheds into railway wagons to be taken to Tiverton and other places. Goodland's of Tiverton ceased using the railway in 1959 when one consignment took three weeks for the journey of 48 miles and arrived in sodden condition because the load had not been covered with tarpaulins.

As the Act prohibited the use of 'locomotives, stationary engines, ropes or "Atmospheric Agency"', the method of working was that in the morning an engine took

Wagons on Totnes Quay.

c. 1924 L.F. Folkard collection

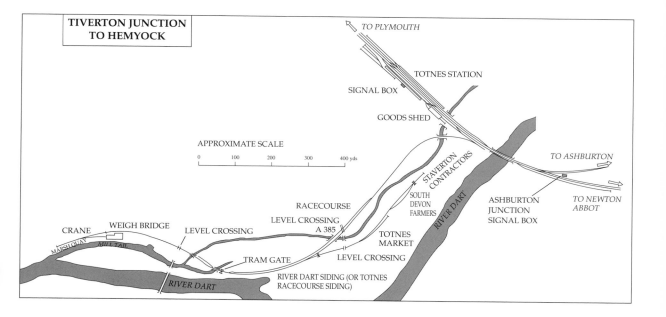

TIVERTON JUNCTION
TO HEMYOCK

TO PLYMOUTH

TOTNES STATION

SIGNAL BOX

GOODS SHED

APPROXIMATE SCALE

0   100   200   300   400 yds

STAVERTON CONTRACTORS

SOUTH
DEVON
FARMERS

RIVER DART

TO ASHBURTON

ASHBURTON
JUNCTION
SIGNAL BOX

TO NEWTON
ABBOT

RACECOURSE
LEVEL CROSSING
A 385

CRANE   WEIGH BRIDGE   LEVEL CROSSING

MARSH QUAY   MILL TAIL

TOTNES
MARKET

TRAM GATE   LEVEL CROSSING

RIVER DART

RIVER DART SIDING (OR TOTNES
RACECOURSE SIDING)

wagons to Tram Gate, a horse then drawing one wagon at a time across the Totnes to Paignton road near Totnes Bridge, a man with a red flag protecting the crossing. About 1950 the horse was replaced by a farm tractor fitted with a front plate and this pushed the wagons. Maximum speed on the locomotive section was limited to 10 m.p.h., raised to 15 m.p.h. in the years following the Second World War, and the load restricted to 35 wagons. The engine collected wagons from Tram Gate in the afternoon. Latterly Great Western Society stock was stored on the branch and on at least one occasion a GWS engine in steam brought wagons up from Tram Gate. The branch closed on 7 December 1969.

Burlescombe station, view Down. A goods train stands in the Up Refuge siding, which gave access to the Westleigh Tramway.

c. 1935 Lens of Sutton

3 ft gauge Bristol & Exeter Railway 0–4–0WT on the timber viaduct, with a Manning Wardle 0–6–0ST below.

1898 Camas UK Ltd

Tramway bridge across the Grand Western Canal, right, and towpath, left.

31.5.94 Author

Westleigh Tramway overbridge, Cracker Corner.

31.5.94 Author

Exeter City Basin signal-box, view Down. The Basin line curves right.

6.8.84 Author

Alphington Road Goods Junction: the City Basin line is on the right, and the Alphington Road Yard on the left.

6.8.84 Author

The asphalt works on the City Basin line.

6.8.84 Author

45 035 and repeater signal, City Basin line.

June 1976 Col. M.H. Cobb

57XX class 0–6–0PT No. 3629 shunting at City Basin.

1.10.58 R.A. Lumber

Sentinel road locomotive No. 5644 *The Elephant* between shunting duties at Teignmouth Quay.
2.8.60 Hugh Ballantyne

14XX class 0–4–2T No. 1466 belonging to the Great Western Society leaves the Down main line at Totnes en route from Buckfastleigh to Totnes Quay.

24.11.65 R.A. Lumber

GWS Open Day. 1366 class 0–6–0PT No. 1369 in steam hauling an auto-coach on the River Dart siding of the Totnes Quay branch. The South Devon Farmers' building is in the background and cattle pens on the right.

9.10.65 R.A. Lumber

No. 1466 with auto-coach on the Totnes Quay branch shunting wagons for BR. View towards the main line.

26.6.65 R.A. Lumber